THE FOUNDATION STONES

THE FOUNDATION STONES

By F. David Fawcett

LAURUS BOOKS

All scripture quotations, unless otherwise indicated, are taken from the HOLY BIBLE, NEW INTERNATIONAL VERSION®, NIV®. Copyright © 1973, 1978, 1984 by International Bible Society. Used by permission of Zondervan. All rights reserved.

Scripture quotations marked NKJV are taken from the New King James Version. Copyright © 1982 by Thomas Nelson, Inc. Used by permission. All rights reserved.

Scripture quotations marked KJV are from the King James Version of the Bible.

THE FOUNDATION STONES
BY F. DAVID FAWCETT

Copyright © 2001-2018 by F. David Fawcett

All rights reserved. This book is protected under the copyright laws of the United States of America. This book may not be copied or reprinted for commercial gain or profit. The use of short quotations or occasional page copying for personal or group study is permitted and encouraged. Permission will be granted on request.

Paperback: ISBN: 978-1-943523-61-0

Mobi (Kindle): ISBN: 978-1-943523-60-3

ePub (iBooks, Nook): ISBN: 978-1-943523-59-7

Published by Laurus Books

LAURUS BOOKS
A DIVISION OF THE LAURUS COMPANY, INC.
www.TheLaurusCompany.com

This book may be purchased in paperback from TheLaurusCompany.com, Amazon.com, and most other retailers around the world. May also be available in formats for electronic readers from their respective stores.

DEDICATION

I remember, many years ago, retreating to my back porch area and weeping before God the Father, asking Him to send a revival to His people. What I was seeing in the body of Christ was not what Jesus died to give us. In fact, in many ways, it looked no different than the world.

As months went by, I felt that the Holy Spirit was leading me to pray for a restoration of the foundation spoken of in Psalms 11:3 (KJV): *"If the foundations be destroyed, what can the righteous do?"*

Over a period of years, the Lord unfolded *The Foundation Stones*.

I dedicate this work

to those possessing hungry hearts,

those who desire to know Christ more intimately

and

to build a foundation that will

stand the test of time.

DISCLAIMER: This book came into being over a span of decades of study. It is possible that some material may have originated in studies from other books or writings and may not have been credited appropriately in this presentation. We apologize if that has happened and, upon notification, will gladly give needed credit where appropriate.

Therefore, leaving the discussion of the
elementary principles of Christ,
let us go on to perfection,
not laying again the foundation of

REPENTANCE FROM DEAD WORKS

and of

FAITH TOWARD GOD,

of

THE DOCTRINE OF BAPTISMS,

of

LAYING ON OF HANDS,

of

RESURRECTION OF THE DEAD,

and of

ETERNAL JUDGMENT.

—Hebrews 6:1-2 NKJV

FOREWORD

I have known Pastor David Fawcett for almost twenty (20) years, and indeed, he is my pastor and friend. I know of the burden that God placed on his heart while pastoring a church in South Carolina almost fifteen years ago. As David prayed and wept every night on his porch pleading with God for revival, he felt the Lord spoke to him that the church did not need a revival but a restoration of the foundation that it was built upon. Out of this encounter with God, and after twelve painstaking years of "living it," *The Foundation Stones* was birthed.

The heart of this book is to equip Christians with a solid biblical salvation followed by an unshakeable understanding of the Word of God. This book is not about denomination or religion, but rather about building a right relationship with God the Father, Jesus Christ our Savior, the Person of the Holy Spirit, and a sound understanding of God's Word.

I challenge you, as I have done, to "try these things and see if they be so." This book will challenge your preset thinking and denominational bent and will draw you to biblical truth.

Although this book is based on only two Scripture verses, Hebrews 6:1 and 2, it includes Scriptures from Genesis to Revelation. If you press in to complete this Bible study, then I will guarantee that you will be able to take every message or sermon or book you receive and see where it fits, or doesn't fit, into these six (6) foundational stones of the Christian faith.

Put down your agendas, choose to be a "lover of the truth," and get ready to experience God …

— Edward C. (Ted) McDonald

TABLE OF CONTENTS

DEDICATION 5
FOREWORD 7
PREFACE 10
INTRODUCTION 11

    The Foundation 12
    The Door to Salvation 16
    Expectations 20
    Discipleship 25
    Principles of Doctrine 34

REPENTANCE FROM DEAD WORKS 37

    Repentance From Dead Works - Introduction 38
    Authority 48
    The Root of Dead Works 54
    Righteousness and Dead Works 59
    Believing the Truth 66
    The Effect of Righteousness 75
    The Deception of Religion 79
    God's Direction vs. My Direction 86

FAITH TOWARD GOD 99

    Faith Toward God - Introduction 100
    Faith's Sight 107
    The Creative Power of God's Word 111
    The Principle of Confession 118
    The Spirit of Faith 125
    The Nearness of God's Word 131
    The Circle of Experience 135
    The Trial of Our Faith 140
    Examining Our Faith 147

TABLE OF CONTENTS Cont'd.

DOCTRINE OF BAPTISMS 153

    Doctrine of Baptisms - Introduction 154
    Baptism Into Repentance 157
    Baptism Into Water 170
    Baptism Into the Holy Spirit 179
    Baptism Into Fire 187
    Baptism Into His Body 193
    Baptism Into Suffering 203
    Baptism Into the Cloud 209

LAYING ON OF HANDS 219

RESURRECTION OF THE DEAD 227

ETERNAL JUDGMENT 237

    Eternal Judgment - Introduction 238
    The Fear of God 246

BIBLIOGRAPHY 251

ABOUT THE AUTHOR 253

PREFACE

The Foundation Stones teaching was inspired by God and designed with a specific purpose in mind. The foundation of our faith, hope, and purpose in this life can only be based on Jesus Christ and His redemption of sinners. Until we understand and put into practice the fundamental truths of our salvation and Christian walk, we are building our lives on shifting sand.

This teaching has been traditionally taught in the timeframe of nine months. It is an investment that should be considered carefully and in the light of the crucial nature of your spiritual growth. You would be hard-pressed to find an individual unwilling to invest nine months to attain the riches of this world. What are the riches of God's purpose and will for your life worth to you?

Finally, consider the sovereignty of God in this instance. You have been introduced to this teaching by a friend most likely, but certainly not by chance. God has ordained this time for YOU, and He has brought you to this point by His divine hand. Do not make the mistake of committing or refusing to commit to this offer on the basis of others. Your response is to God alone, and it may be that what is at stake is a life-transforming encounter with the Truth.

Our goal is not to get through this teaching. It is HOW we go through it that will determine the degree of discipleship we attain! The result of this teaching will not be an impressive "building" but rather a solid foundation upon which to build.

> *"Consider carefully what you hear," he continued. "With the measure you use, it will be measured to you—and even more."* —Mark 4:21-29 (v. 24)

INTRODUCTION

The Foundation Stones
Introduction

THE FOUNDATION

The first and most important step in your Christian walk is ensuring a solid foundation in Jesus Christ. The verses below outline the six components of this foundation, which are the basis of the entire teaching upon which you are about to embark. There are several fallacies commonly believed regarding the matter of our foundational stability. The following points dispel these assumptions.

- **The length of time you have been a Christian is not an indication of the quality of your foundation.**

- **A good foundation is not built on how much Scripture you KNOW but how much Scripture is APPLIED to your life.**

> *"For though by this time you ought to be teachers, you need someone to teach you again the first principles of the oracles of God; and you have come to need milk and not solid food. For everyone who partakes only of milk is unskilled in the word of righteousness, for he is a babe. But solid food belongs to those who are of full age, that is, those who by reason of use have their senses exercised to discern both good and evil. Therefore, leaving the discussion of the elementary principles of Christ, let us go on to perfection, not laying again the foundation of* **REPENTANCE FROM DEAD WORKS** *and of* **FAITH TOWARD GOD,** *of* **THE DOCTRINE OF BAPTISMS,** *of* **LAYING ON OF HANDS,** *of* **RESURRECTION OF THE DEAD,** *and of* **ETERNAL JUDGMENT."**
>
> —Hebrews 5:12 - 6:2 NKJV (emphasis added)

The Foundation Stones
Introduction

"Do not merely listen to the word, and so deceive yourselves. Do what it says." —James 1:19-25 (v. 22)

"If anyone wills to do His will ..." —John 7:17 (NKJV)

"Therefore everyone who hears these words of mine and puts them into practice is like a wise man who built his house on the rock."
—Matthew 7:24

The question I must ask myself is not "Do I KNOW this truth?" but "Am I DOING this truth?"

- **As is true in the law of nature, what you sow spiritually you will also reap spiritually when speaking of building a foundation.**

"Do not be deceived: God cannot be mocked. A man reaps what he sows. Whoever sows to please their flesh, from the flesh will reap destruction; whoever sows to please the Spirit, from the Spirit will reap eternal life." —Galatians 6:7-9

- **If we fall after we have been born again, we have a deficiency in our foundation. Through these experiences, God is exposing the deficiencies in order to reveal the truth.**

"If you hold to my teaching, you are really my disciples. Then you will know the truth, and the truth will set you free." —John 8:31-32

The Foundation Stones
Introduction

The foundations built in many churches today have two main deficiencies. Not only do these deficiencies hinder our walk with Christ, they often render it useless because we do not understand God's heart for us nor His will for our lives. These two deficiencies are:

- **Foundations not founded on a personal love relationship with Jesus Christ, but rather on WORKS.**

    Churches often take our initial small flame of desire for God and apply it to works instead of allowing the Lord to consume and strengthen it.

- **Foundations not built on DISCIPLESHIP (the "deeper life").**

    Christ built His church on disciples.

Questions to ask yourself:

Why does God love me?

_____

_____

Who am I?

_____

_____

What is my purpose in life?

_____

_____

The Foundation Stones
Introduction

Spend one-half hour with Jesus each day. Go before the Lord for nothing else but Him. Read the following scriptures for understanding of His heart for you.

Psalm 100	(expressing our gratitude for His love)
Psalm 91	(understanding our relationship with God)
Psalm 149	(worshipping God)
Psalm 63	(describing His consuming love)
Psalm 23	(describing His protective love)

NOTES:

The Foundation Stones
Introduction

THE DOOR TO SALVATION

> *"Most assuredly, I say to you, he who does not enter the sheepfold by the door, but climbs up some other way, the same is a thief and a robber. But he who enters by the door is the shepherd of the sheep. To him the doorkeeper opens, and the sheep hear his voice; and he calls his own sheep by name and leads them out. And when he brings out his own sheep, he goes before them; and the sheep follow him, for they know his voice. Yet they will by no means follow a stranger, but will flee from him, for they do not know the voice of strangers ...* **I am the door of the sheep."**
> — John 10:1-7 (NKJV)

The basis of Christianity is a personal love relationship with Jesus. The verses listed here spell out the fact that Jesus is the **one and only** way to eternal life, a relationship with the Father, and a victorious Christian walk.

In John 14:6 (NKJV), Jesus says, *"I am the* **way***, the* **truth***, and the* **life***. No one comes to the Father except through* **Me***."* That is to say that Jesus is the only way to all that we were created for. He himself is both everything that our hearts long for as well as the door to it. Until we come to Jesus on these terms—believing that He is the only hope we have and the only hope we need—then we will never experience God's purpose for our lives.

> *"For no one can lay any foundation other than the one already laid, which is Jesus Christ."* —1 Corinthians 3:11

> *"Therefore everyone who hears these words of mine and puts them into practice is like a wise man who built his house on the rock."*
> —Matthew 7:24

The Foundation Stones
Introduction

"You study the Scriptures diligently because you think that in them you have eternal life. These are the very Scriptures that testify about me, yet you refuse to come to me to have life."

—John 5:39-40

THE PLAN OF SALVATION

Throughout the Bible, we are given keys to understanding God's plan of salvation for His people. Although the following verses may be familiar to you already, it is important that you consider them carefully for yourself and others. Not only will a clear understanding of this process give you a sense of security about your own faith, but it will allow you to lead others to Christ and/or to disciple them.

The last words of Jesus on this earth, the Great Commission, emphasize the significance of this assignment. He said, *"Go into all the world and preach the gospel to all creation"* (see Mark 16:14-20). Would He have saved these instructions for His triumphal departure had they not been extremely important?

Determine to spend some time looking up and meditating on the verses following to prepare for whatever God may have in store for you as His witness to the world. Cross-reference these Scriptures in your Bible so that you can easily walk someone through the steps when the time comes. And ask God to help you develop a game plan with these key truths.

The Foundation Stones
Introduction

We all need to be born again.

"Jesus answered, 'Very truly I tell you, no one can enter the kingdom of God unless they are born of water and the Spirit.' " (v.5) **John 3:1-21**

"[F]or all have sinned and fall short of the glory of God." **Romans 3:23**

"There is no one righteous, not even one." **Romans 3:10-11**

"The heart is deceitful above all things and beyond cure."
Jeremiah 17:9-10

"All of us have become like one who is unclean, and all our righteous acts are like filthy rags." **Isaiah 64:6**

"We all, like sheep, have gone astray, each of us has turned to our own way." **Isaiah 53:6**

We are unable to save ourselves.

"[K]now that a man is not justified by observing the law, but by faith in Jesus Christ." **Galatians 2:16**

"For whoever keeps the whole law and yet stumbles at just one point is guilty of breaking all of it." **James 2:10**

"There is a way that seems right to a man, but in the end it leads to death."
Proverbs 14:12

"[H]e saved us, not because of righteous things we had done, but because of his mercy" **Titus 3:5**

"Salvation is found in no one else, for there is no other name under heaven given to men by which we must be saved." **Acts 4:12**

The Foundation Stones
Introduction

We are born again by believing, repenting, and receiving Him.

"Believe in the Lord Jesus, and you will be saved." **Acts 16:30-31**

"Yet to all who received him, to those who believed in his name, he gave the right to become children of God—" **John 1:12**

"[W]hoever hears my word and believes him who sent me has eternal life and will not be judged but has crossed over from death to life." **John 5:24**

"Repent, then, and turn to God, so that your sins may be wiped out" **Acts 3:19**

"If you declare with your mouth, 'Jesus is Lord,' and believe in your heart that God raised him from the dead, you will be saved." **Romans 10:9-13**

"Whoever acknowledges me before others, I will also acknowledge him before my Father in heaven." **Matthew 10:32-33**

"Go into all the world and preach the gospel to all creation." **Mark 16:15-18**

Salvation is a free gift to all.

"Christ Jesus came into the world to save sinners" **1 Timothy 1:15**

"He himself bore our sins in his body ... by his wounds you have been healed." **1 Peter 2:24**

"[S]o that by the grace of God he might taste death for everyone." **Hebrews 2:9**

"For Christ died for sins once for all, the righteous for the unrighteous, to bring you to God." **1 Peter 3:18**

"For God so loved the world that he gave his one and only Son, that whoever believes in him shall not perish but have eternal life." **John 3:16**

The Foundation Stones
Introduction

EXPECTATIONS

Before we begin our study of the foundation stones of the Christian faith, we must first come to an understanding of what to expect throughout this teaching. The following are the basic elements of receiving and growing in truth.

PRAYER

If you are studying this book in a class setting, the teacher assumes the responsibility of praying over the disciples and the principles that are taught. The disciple must, in turn, pray for his or her own heart. It is important to realize that God is the *"author and finisher of our faith"* (Hebrews 12:2 NKJV), which means that we must come to Him for even the desire to follow and obey, not to mention the power. It is not a matter of willpower but of God's ability to save us in every way. With that in mind, make it a priority to seek God specifically about your reception of this material on a weekly, if not daily, basis. As Psalm 119:18 says, I must ask God to open my eyes to His truth, *"Open my eyes that I may see wonderful things in your law."*

FAITHFULNESS

While a teacher commits to being faithful to each disciple in the preparation and presentation of the material, the disciple must also make a commitment to be faithful through OBEDIENCE, CONSISTENCY, and PARTICIPATION. Below are some practical guidelines for doing this:

Study as consistently as possible.

> Because each lesson in this teaching is essentially a building block in the foundation of God's Word, getting behind with your study will be a hindrance as the course progresses. Consistency will prove to be very important.

The Foundation Stones
Introduction

Keep a notebook for taking and studying notes.

> Taking notes throughout this study is essential. Not only is it impossible to digest all of the truth that is communicated, but it is also very difficult to hold onto a newly-revealed truth if it is not written down. God's desire is to penetrate the world **YOU** live in with these truths, and diligent study and meditation on them is often the vehicle He uses. Notetaking leaves a trail, so to speak, which you can easily follow or share with others.

Do what is instructed.

> Remember that the key to this teaching is not KNOWING the truth, but DOING it. When you are presented with a challenge, instruction, or suggestion, do not be quick to shrug it off because it is a familiar concept. If you cannot testify to its power in your life currently, then it probably means that you are not DOING it! Do not deceive yourself. Instead, be quick to obey and open to receive whatever God has for you.

TRUTH

While a teacher has the responsibility of speaking the truth of God's Word as the Holy Spirit directs, the disciple also has a responsibility to the truth. He or she must seek God for **REVELATION** of His Word. When the Holy Spirit reveals a truth to someone, it becomes LIFE to them, not just knowledge. First Corinthians 8:1 tells us that *"knowledge puffs up,"* which is the reason we see so many Christians with head-knowledge but no revelation or life.

There are three basic steps we must take if a truth is to become real to us in our everyday lives:

The Foundation Stones
Introduction

1. REVELATION

Receiving understanding of some truth
by the revelation of the Holy Spirit.

The natural mind will never comprehend the things of the Spirit unless He quickens them to you.

> *"[That God] may give to you the spirit of wisdom and revelation in the knowledge of Him, the eyes of your understanding being enlightened."*
> —Ephesians 1:17-18 (NKJV)

2. TRANSFORMATION

Experiencing a heart-change as you
hold onto/possess the truth.

When we hold onto the truth, it begins to transform our minds, which is followed by a change in the way we view ourselves, God, and the world around us.

> *"Do not conform any longer to the pattern of this world, but be transformed by the renewing of your mind."* —Romans 12:1-2

3. MANIFESTATION

Being led and motivated by the truth—
the truth possesses me.

Once we determine to possess a truth and walk in the light of it, that same truth begins to possess us. As we DO the Word of God, it will manifest in our day-to-day reality, and we will witness its healing work in our lives.

> *"The Word became flesh."* —John 1:14

The Foundation Stones
Introduction

A clear explanation of this principle is found in the book of Matthew where Jesus speaks about the effects of revelation on our lives. When the process above is followed and truth is manifested in a person, more life and revelation is given. On the other hand, a heart that turns from the truth will be hardened to the things of God, and the revelation will be taken away—maybe never to be given again. This scripture is as much a warning to the lukewarm as it is a promise to the faithful.

> *"He replied, 'The knowledge of the secrets of the kingdom of heaven has been given to you, but not to them. Whoever has will be given more, and he will have an abundance. Whoever does not have, even what he has will be taken from him. This is why I speak in parables:*
>
> *"Though seeing, they do not see; though hearing, they do not hear or understand."*
>
> *In them is fulfilled the prophecy of Isaiah:*
>
> *"You will ever be hearing but never understanding; you will ever be seeing but never perceiving. For this people's heart has become callused; they hardly hear with their ears, and they have closed their eyes. Otherwise they might see with their eyes, hear with their ears, understand with their hearts and turn, and I would heal them."*
> —Matthew 13:11-15

There is also an illustration given by Jesus on this subject in Luke 8:4-15, The Parable of the Sower. God is presented to us as the Sower, and the seed represents revelation of truth given by God to His children. While it is true that God deals with each of us individually, giving us revelation in different ways and in His perfect timing, this parable leads us to understand that we are all susceptible to the same pitfalls in our Christian walk. We see that revelation is lost in a number of different ways—being entangled in the cares and worries of this world or lacking a solid foundation. Luke 8:15

The Foundation Stones
Introduction

describes the "good soil" as the one who simply holds onto the "seed" and allows God to produce a crop. Holding onto and walking in obedience to the truth is our only responsibility in God's field.

> *"But the seed on good soil stands for those with a noble and good heart, who hear the word, retain it, and by persevering produce a crop."* —Luke 8:15

> The only truths that will eventually grip me at the core of my being are the truths by which I consistently live.

The thing to remember when considering your investment in this relationship with the living God is that He created you for a purpose—a divine purpose. True success in the eyes of God is the extent to which you allow His life to flow through you. We are not called to be imitators of Jesus, and we are not merely required to pass on a message. God desires to pass it on THROUGH us. Only God can bring life to a dead and dying world. In John 6:53, Jesus tells his disciple that *"unless you eat the flesh of the Son of Man and drink his blood, you have no life in you."* God's purpose for you is the life of Jesus lived through you and overflowing to others.

Consider the following questions before you continue in this study:

- *Can people see Christ in me?*

- *Do I have the tools I need to release others into the fullness of the vision of God for their lives?*

> Christ does not just give us a message. He makes us the message.

The Foundation Stones
Introduction

DISCIPLESHIP

We have used the word "disciple" several times already in the introduction of this teaching. Most likely, this term has been filed somewhere between **student** and **follower** in your mental vocabulary. It may interest you to know, however, that this word was used to describe the believers of Jesus two-hundred-fifty times in the New Testament, whereas the word "Christian" appears only three times! (See Acts 11:26.)

Furthermore, the Great Commission (the last words of Jesus on this earth, found in Matthew 28:18-20) instructs us to *"go and make disciples of all nations."* While God gives His people the desire to know and follow Him, we (Christ's church) have been given the responsibility of "making disciples." In the plan of God for the maturing of our faith, His disciples are to disciple others. Although instruction plays a part in this process, living the example of a victorious life for others to imitate is the unique **fathering** aspect of discipleship. See 2 Timothy 2:2, 15 for examples of Paul's instruction to Timothy as his spiritual father. First Corinthians 4:15-16 (NKJV) says, *"For though you might have ten thousand instructors in Christ, yet you do not have many fathers."*

When we consider the church of today, it is interesting to refer to the book of Acts in which the New Testament church had a hand in the making of disciples by the multitudes (see Acts 6:1-4, 7). One might be prone to wondering why we do not see this happening today, but only until they understand the cost of becoming a disciple of Christ.

The Bible has much to say about the cost of becoming a disciple, and there is no pretending that it is the comfortable road to take. But the alternative is much worse than discomfort; it is never seeing the fulfillment of God's purpose for us as believers. Considering this, we would do well to come to grips with the significance of this term and evaluate our own relationship with Jesus Christ in the light of this standard set long ago.

The Foundation Stones
   Introduction

THE DISTINGUISHING MARK OF A DISCIPLE

> *"Many will say to me on that day, 'Lord, Lord, did we not prophesy in your name and in your name drive out demons and in your name perform many miracles?' Then I will tell them plainly, 'I never knew you. Away from me, you evildoers!'"* —Matthew 7:22-23

We must learn to identify a true disciple in the eyes of God. Above is a quotation of Jesus recorded in the book of Matthew that is often troubling. If we take these words to heart, we will begin to wonder what distinguishes a true disciple from the "evildoers" Jesus speaks of.

The keys to understanding this verse are found in two places. First, it is important to note that Jesus does not cast them out because of what they did or did not DO but because there was no relationship between Himself and them. God does not call us to **perform** our way to heaven. We must KNOW Jesus Christ if we are to legitimately call Him "Lord." The second thing to take note of is the verse preceding these two. Jesus says in Matthew 7:21, "Not everyone who says to me, 'Lord, Lord,' will enter the kingdom of heaven, but only he who does the will of my Father who is in heaven." Although this may appear to refer to **works**, there is a subtle but dramatic difference.

> *"Whoever has my commands and keeps them is the one who loves me. The one who loves me will be loved by my Father, and I too will love them and show myself to them."* —John 14:21

If you look closely at this verse, you will see the connection between relationship and obedience. Jesus is telling us that obedience is the natural result—and thus the proof—of a loving relationship with God and Christ. We are never rejected because we fail to DO but because we cast God aside in our determination to make it on our own. We are designed to be motivated by His love in all things. The most important question we have to face is one that Jesus asked His disciples: *"Who do you say I am?"* (Matthew 16:15). Who is Jesus to you?

So we come to the true disciple—who has both a loving relationship with Jesus Christ as well as the desire and discipline to walk obediently out of nothing but love for God. This is where the teaching and learning come in, and where most people are abandoned to their own devices. *The Foundation Stones* teaching, however, was designed with this very purpose in mind.

A DISCIPLE can be defined as a "disciplined learner." [6]

THE HEART OF A DISCIPLE

The heart of a disciple is one that gives Christ first place. We can look at this in the light of our daily time spent in the Word and in prayer. Everything in the world poses as a distraction to our commitment to Jesus Christ. Do we still put Him first?

> *"If anyone comes to me and does not hate his father and mother, wife and children, brothers and sisters —yes, even his own life—he cannot be my disciple ... those of you who does not give up everything you have cannot be my disciples."* —See Luke 14:25-33 (vs. 26, 33)

In the previous Scripture reference, Jesus' words leave no room for guessing. He goes out of His way to emphasize the importance of putting Him before everything and everybody who is dear to us. But He does not stop there. He also tells us that we must hate our own life in order to be His disciples. The following verses speak the same warning to us:

> *"For whoever wants to save his life will lose it, but whoever loses his life for me will save it."* —Luke 9:24

> *"The man who loves his life will lose it, while the man who hates his life in this world will keep it for eternal life."* —John 12:25

The Foundation Stones
Introduction

THE "CROSS" OF A DISCIPLE

"And whoever does not carry their cross and follow me cannot be my disciple." —Luke 14:27

Taking up the cross is a requirement for being a disciple of Christ. The cross marked the place of death for Jesus in the literal sense, and it is similarly set before us as our goal in this life, only in a different way. We are called to die to ourselves (specifically, our own desires, rights, and agendas) and surrender our wills to God on a daily basis.

In 1 John 2:15 we are told, *"Do not love the world or anything in the world."* This leads us to the other aspect of the cross in our lives. We are called to be separate from and **dead to** the world around us. In the book of Galatians, Paul expresses this concept very well:

"May I never boast except in the cross of our Lord Jesus Christ, through which the world has been crucified to me, and I to the world."
—Galatians 6:14

It may seem strange to us that we are encouraged to view the world with such contempt because, after all, there appear to be many good things about this life. But we are informed in James 4:4 that *"anyone who chooses to be a friend of the world becomes an enemy of God."* The following verse sheds more light on the reason that this is true:

"We know that we are children of God, and that the whole world is under the control of the evil one." —1 John 5:19

Therefore, if we belong to God, we are no longer players on the game board of the "evil one." The world itself is under his control, and we are set apart as servants of God. Paul says that *"you have been set free from sin and have become slaves of God"* (Romans 6:22). The identity we share with the cross of Christ is one of death but also one of resurrection. We have been ransomed from this world into the Kingdom of God, and our most difficult but important task is to count ourselves daily as His.

The Foundation Stones
Introduction

THE COST OF BEING A DISCIPLE

Before we choose to become a disciple of Christ, we must first count the cost. The Bible is filled with practical wisdom and guidance for everyday life as well as spiritual matters. Luke recorded some words of wisdom spoken by Jesus regarding the cost of discipleship. In Luke 14:28-32, Jesus speaks about the wisdom of the man who estimates the cost of building a house or going into battle as examples before the matter is decided in his mind, and He warns against the foolishness of making rash decisions. Then He compares these scenarios with that of counting the cost of discipleship, saying, *"In the same way, those of you who do not give up everything you have cannot be my disciples"* (Luke 14:33).

Discipleship is not a popular lifestyle, and rightly so. But for those of us who choose this lifestyle, discipleship brings with it the promise of life, hope, fulfillment, and joy that are foreign to this world. The apostle Paul may have said it best in this verse:

> *"But whatever were gains to me I now consider loss for the sake of Christ. What is more, I consider everything a loss because of the surpassing worth of knowing Christ Jesus my Lord, for whose sake I have lost all things. I consider them garbage, that I may gain Christ and be found in him, not having a righteousness of my own that comes from the law, but that which is through faith in Christ—the righteousness that comes from God on the basis of faith. I want to know Christ—yes, to know the power of his resurrection and participation in his sufferings, becoming like him in his death, and so, somehow, attaining to the resurrection from the dead."*
> —Philippians 3:7-11

The Foundation Stones
  Introduction

THE PURPOSE OF BEING A DISCIPLE

Our purpose as disciples is to learn our identity in Christ and walk in it. God's Word clearly and repeatedly warns us about the schemes of the enemy in our lives. Satan's greatest deception occurs in the minds of the children of God. As long as he can keep us ignorant of our identity in Christ, we will allow ourselves to be stolen from and believe we are paupers. Some Christians never realize that God has made them rich (peace, hope, joy, etc), and they struggle through each day as victims of this world. But the disciple walks in the authority God has given and in victory. How are we to reclaim what has been stolen from us if we do not know what it is and what right we have to it?

The prophet Isaiah gives us a vivid picture of what the enemy has done to God's children and His church as a whole:

> *"For he says: 'By the strength of my hand I have done this, and by my wisdom, because I have understanding. I removed the boundaries of nations, I plundered their treasures; like a mighty one I subdued their kings. As one reaches into a nest, so my hand reached for the wealth of the nations; as people gather abandoned eggs, so I gathered all the countries; not one flapped a wing, or opened its mouth to chirp.'"*
> —Isaiah 10:12-14

We are told here that Satan has essentially removed our boundaries as the people of God so that we no longer know what is ours. Not only is this the case, but we also find that he has targeted our foundations, which has left us with nothing to stand on:

> *"When the foundations are being destroyed, what can the righteous do?"* —Psalm 11:3

Our tendency as humans is to fear what we cannot see, and especially the spiritual forces of evil that are bent on destroying God's people. We can

The Foundation Stones
Introduction

recognize Satan's handiwork in our lives, and we wonder why he has the power he does. Christians do not fail because of a lack of God's power to save them. We are not vulnerable to the enemy unless we choose to be ignorant to the truth of God's Word.

We are told in 2 Peter 1:3, *"His divine power has given us everything we need for a godly life."* But it finishes with a condition: *"through our knowledge of him who called us by his own glory and goodness."* We must KNOW Him deeply and understand His heart for us in order to stand.

And it is important to recognize that God is "mighty to save." When we are tempted to fear the enemy, we need to recall the words of the prophet Isaiah:

> *"The Lord Almighty is the one you are to regard as holy, he is the one you are to fear, he is the one you are to dread. He will be a holy place."*
> —Isaiah 8:13-14

In the book of Isaiah, God also speaks of the security, strength, and life that a foundation in Christ promises. God has a way of exposing and replacing defective parts of our foundations, and He is faithful to do this for those who have chosen to sit at His feet in discipleship.

> *"See, I lay a stone in Zion, a tested stone, a precious cornerstone for a sure foundation; the one who relies on it will never be stricken with panic. ... hail will sweep away your refuge, the lie, and water will overflow your hiding place."* —Isaiah 28:16-17

FURTHER STUDY

Read Hebrews 5:12 – 6:2

Memorize the six foundational stones and the verse reference.

The Foundation Stones
Introduction

SHADOW vs. SUBSTANCE

> *"In fact, though by this time you ought to be teachers, you need someone to teach you the elementary truths of God's word all over again."* —Hebrews 5:12

In the book of Hebrews, Paul introduces the "foundation stones" of the Christian faith with the exhortation to the Hebrew believers that is quoted above. We can conclude by Paul's statement that maturity in our walk with Christ does not necessarily come with time. Just as with the Hebrews whom Paul addressed in this verse, we can remain as spiritual **babies** for as long as we choose. Maturity in Christ comes only through the WORD and EXPERIENCE working together.

God's Word is "living and active" in the spiritual sense. It was created to cut through, to set free, and to give life. In short, it is to be experienced. When it is not, it becomes as common and lifeless as the things of this world. Why is this the case for most people? It is because we do not LIVE the truth. In John 7:17, Jesus says, *"Anyone who chooses to do the will of God will find out whether my teaching comes from God or whether I speak on my own."* And in John 8:31-32, Jesus tells believers, *"If you hold to my teaching, you are really my disciples. Then you will know the truth, and the truth will set you free."* As we CHOOSE to walk in the truth (the Word of God), we begin to experience it.

In Colossians 2:16-17, Paul refers to the things of this world (namely religious traditions) as SHADOWS, to be compared with the SUBSTANCE, or reality, found only in Christ:

> *"These are a shadow of the things that were to come; the reality, however, is found in Christ."* —Colossians 2:17

Many of us have settled for the shadows, but God draws us to hunger and thirst for the substance. He knows, and we should know by now, too, that the shadows never satisfy. Their purpose is to point us to reality, which is found only in Him.

The Foundation Stones
Introduction

Oftentimes, Jesus used the phrase: *"He who has ears, let him hear,"* which is an important directive for us. In saying, "he who has ears," Jesus is implying that only those who have a relationship with God have been given ears to hear Him (by the Holy Spirit). The phrase, "let him hear," tells us something even more important, that hearing God is a choice we must make. We may not be accustomed to hearing and following our Shepherd, but, as believers, we all have the ability and the responsibility to do so.

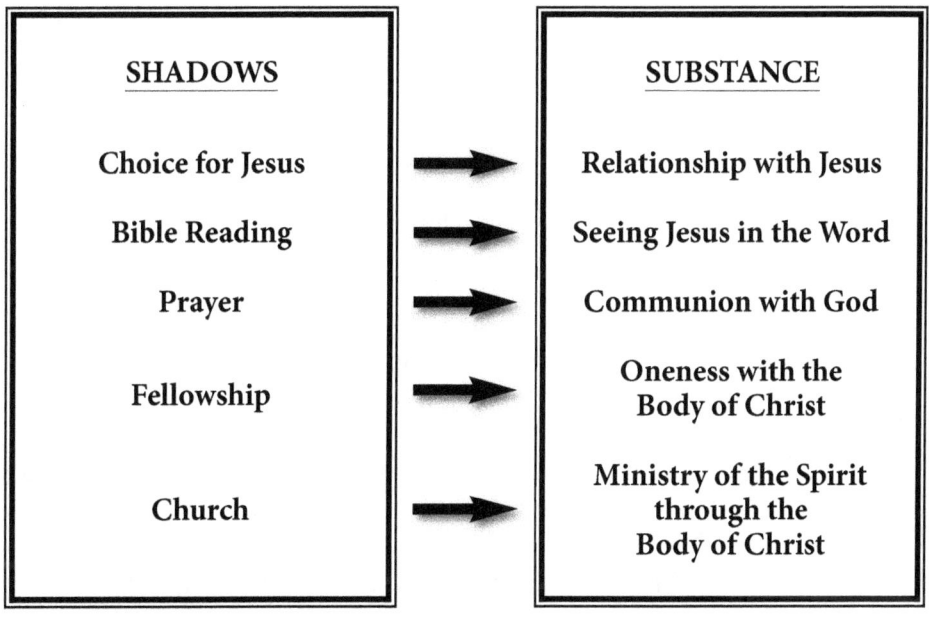

The shadows are not innately bad or harmful. They are necessary to lead us to the substance. Consider how this compares to marriage. There is a necessary legal aspect of becoming husband and wife, but we would be foolish to believe that marriage was no more than the ceremony itself. A marriage is a living, growing connection between two people, and it is to be lived and experienced every day. In short, it is the earthly model of God's desired relationship with us. We can be a child of God technically and live in the coldness of the shadows all of our lives just as a couple can be married by law but never experience a loving relationship. In both cases, what is lost is the purpose behind it all.

The Foundation Stones
Introduction

PRINCIPLES OF DOCTRINE

The word "Principle" is defined as "Chief, first in rank or person" and is translated "beginning, corner, power, principality and rule."
          (Strongs #746 – root *Arche*).[5]

The word "Doctrine" is defined as "Something said (including thought), reasoning, computation, divine expression" and is translated "Word."
          (Strongs #3056 – root *Logos*).[5]

In this teaching, it is important to recognize the significance of the term "Principles of Doctrine" as it relates to the foundational building blocks of our faith. In several places, the Bible refers to Christ Himself as **THE**:

    "Chief Cornerstone"   (Ephesians 2:20, 1 Peter 2:6-7)
    "Capstone"   (Matthew 21:42)
    "Foundation"   (1 Corinthians 3:10-15)

And the doctrine (or reasoning) behind the foundational truths taught here is the **Word**—inspired by God and having final authority in all things. So we see that they work hand-in-hand. The **principles** are founded in Christ Himself, Who is the foundation of our faith, and the **doctrine** spoken by God in His Word is the means by which that foundation is established. This verse ties these two aspects together in one illustration:

> *"Therefore everyone who hears these words of mine and puts them into practice is like a wise man who built his house on the rock. The rain came down, the streams rose, and the winds blew and beat against that house; yet it did not fall, because it had its foundation on the rock. But everyone who hears these words of mine and does not put them into practice is like a foolish man who built his house on sand. The rain came down, the streams rose, and the winds blew and beat against that house, and it fell with a great crash."*
>   —Matthew 7:24-27

The Foundation Stones
Introduction

We refer to the foundation stones as the "Principles of Doctrine" because they are the basis through which all truth is filtered. Any teaching from the Word of God can be tied into the truths listed below. They make up our foundation, the foundation on which all other things are built. Not only is this important to keep in perspective when going through this study, but it is also a tool for deciphering the truth in any situation. Remember that the Word of God is the standard by which to measure all thoughts, teachings, and beliefs. Never default to any other source.

The Foundation Stones
(Hebrews 5:12 – 6:2)

- **Repentance from Dead Works**

- **Faith Toward God**

- **The Doctrine of Baptisms**

- **Laying on of Hands**

- **Resurrection of the Dead**

- **Eternal Judgment**

The Foundation Stones
Introduction

NOTES:

REPENTANCE FROM DEAD WORKS

REPENTANCE FROM DEAD WORKS

INTRODUCTION

At last, we have come to the foundation stones of our faith, and the first element of this teaching (as found in Hebrew 5:12 – 6:2) is termed "Repentance from Dead." The words repentance and sin are commonly used in our culture, but do we really understand what they mean? If not, we are probably not familiar with the term dead works either. And this brings us to a good starting point—understanding what sin is.

SIN

Contrary to popular belief, sin is NOT what we do. It is not the curse word, the mean thought, or the spiteful act.

SIN IS WHO WE ARE APART FROM GOD.

Take, for instance, the example of the rich young man who approached Jesus with the question, *"[W]hat good thing must I do to get eternal life?"* (see Matthew 19:16-30). Jesus replied with a handful of commandments, all of which the man professed to keep. Then Jesus spoke to the very thing that was separating him from God—his riches. The issue was not anything he had done or even the riches that he possessed, **but the fact that his riches possessed him**. He was dependent on worldly things and therefore independent from God.

Maybe you are thinking, "This is one warning in the Bible that does not apply to me. I don't have any riches to depend on." But stop a minute to consider what you ARE depending on. If it is not God, then it is something or somebody else. What in your life (material possession or otherwise) do you feel you could never live without? That is the thing that God is pointing to. Let's face it, no matter how good or noble our intentions in life, we are in the same boat as the rich young man as long as we are apart from God in any area.

SIN is living a life independent from God.

If you are like most people (even most Christians), you know that something inside of you struggles against the idea of **DEPENDENCE** on anything or anybody. It is not a popular goal in today's culture, especially not in America. We are completely dependent on others when we come into this world, but we are rewarded for and encouraged toward more independence as we grow up. It is against our nature to remain dependent, even on God.

The truth, however, is that we were created to be dependent on our Father for all things. You may wonder how all of this fits together in God's plan, and maybe the next section, which touches on dead works will shed some light on the matter.

DEAD WORKS

The institution of **Religion** by men has created a harmful misconception within the Church of Jesus Christ as a whole. Religion teaches that we are to keep a set of rules in order to be accepted and used by God and that the breaking of one of these is a sin committed. Early in our Christianity, we are placed on the treadmill of **works** and frustrated by our lack of power to do the "right thing." Who has never read verses like *"Be holy, because I am holy"* (1 Peter 1:16) and wondered how God can expect so much from us?

Philippians 2:13 tells us, *"for it is God who works in you to will and to act in order to fulfill his good purpose."* We are also told that the Word of God is *"at work in you who believe"* (1 Thessalonians 2:13). Can you see the point that Paul is trying to make? **God is at work in us**—to the extent that we allow Him—**doing the very things He expects of us!** God knows better than we do that we are weak-willed and unable to walk uprightly as Jesus did. He is not interested in our best efforts, but in our willingness to be nothing more than a vessel. **It is no longer a matter of *DOING FOR GOD* but of allowing God to do through us.**

The Foundation Stones
Repentance From Dead Works

Isaiah the prophet made many statements, such as the one below, which speak of our hopeless condition apart from Christ:

> *"But we are all like an unclean thing, and all our righteousnesses are like filthy rags; we all fade as a leaf, and our iniquities, like the wind, have taken us away."* —Isaiah 64:6 (NKJV)

The Bible makes it clear that every work we produce apart from God is **dead**; hence, the term **"Dead Works."** It can be nothing more, for it is coming from a dead source. Only the Holy Spirit living in us gives us spiritual life, through which come **Living Works**. Why do I need to be dependent on God for all things? Because I can never do the works of God. But the works of God can be done **through me** when I depend on Him.

And so we are faced with a bit of a paradox. In life, we strive to get BETTER at things as we practice them. In a growing walk with Christ, we never get better; we just get better at allowing God to work through us as we depend on Him and stand on the truth. Those of you who believe you must become **good enough** for God to use you will find nothing but frustration. God will continually bring you back to the realization that you can do nothing apart from Him. The apostle Paul wrote these words:

> *"I know that good itself does not dwell in me, that is, in my sinful nature. For I have the desire to do what is good, but I cannot carry it out ... What a wretched man I am! Who will rescue me from this body that is subject to death?"* —Romans 7:18-25

The man who authored the majority of the New Testament books is testifying to his wretched condition. What should that tell us about our own? Paul knew the power and heart of God better than any of us, and yet he never lost sight of his weakness apart from God. If you are still skeptical, consider the words Jesus (God Incarnate) spoke about His own dependence on His Father:

> *"Very truly I tell you, the Son can do nothing by himself; he can do only what he sees his Father doing, because whatever the Father does the Son also does."* —John 5:17-24

> *"The words I say to you I do not speak on my own authority. Rather, it is the Father, living in me, who is doing his work."*
> —John 14:10

Make no mistake. We have nothing to offer God but a willingness to be used by Him. Our purpose in God's economy is to grow in dependence on Him. When we do this, we become righteous-conscious instead of sin-conscious, meaning that we begin to be more conscious of the righteousness of Christ working within us than of our sinful nature. We are privileged instruments of His grace to the world around us, and the Bible says that God even credits TO US the good works that **He** is solely responsible for producing within us.

> *"[L]et your light shine before others, that they may see your good deeds and glorify your Father in heaven."* —Matthew 5:16

And even more astounding is the statement Jesus made in John 14:12: *"Very truly I tell you, whoever believes in me will do the works I have been doing, and they will do even greater things than these, because I am going to the Father."* God's desire is to impact the world through us as He did through Jesus, and to an even greater extent. Our only responsibility is to allow Him.

REPENTANCE

Because the concept of repentance is often misunderstood, our first endeavor is to clarify the meaning of the term. We will refer to this verse as our starting point:

> *"Godly sorrow brings repentance that leads to salvation and leaves no regret, but worldly sorrow brings death."* —2 Corinthians 7:10

The Foundation Stones
Repentance From Dead Works

In 2 Corinthians 7:10, Paul identifies two types of **sorrow**, one of which leads to repentance and salvation, and the other leads to death. We may be quick to assume that "godly sorrow" pertains to those who are believers while "worldly sorrow" is exclusive to unbelievers. In part, this is true, for those who do not know God **cannot** experience godly sorrow. However, many children of God do not experience it either, but only because they choose not to.

Pay close attention to the differences between the definitions as found in *Strongs Concordance* (#3341 and #3338 respectively):

Godly Sorrow

Repent (Metanoia) – reversal of decision, to change one's mind. From root words **meta**, denoting accompaniment amid, and **noica**, to exercise the mind, observe, to comprehend, heed to, perceive, understand.[5]

Worldly Sorrow

Repented (Metamellomai) – to regret afterwards, to regret (because of consequences). From root words **meta**, denoting accompaniment amid, and **melo**, to be of interest, to concern, it matters to oneself.[5]

Worldly sorrow, in a nutshell, is *regret that comes due to the consequences of an action*, whether those consequences are shame, punishment, or guilt. Many people associate repentance with emotional shows and/or attempts to *make up for* a wrong (as with many religious rites and ordinances). Neither of these is true repentance, but rather **PENANCE**, punishing oneself, in a sense. And the motive in these instances is always to relieve the conscience. A good example of this is found in the account of Judas Iscariot's response to Jesus' death sentence. Shortly after this, the Bible tells us that Judas hanged himself, no doubt overwhelmed by the guilt he felt:

> *"When Judas, who had betrayed him, saw that Jesus was condemned, he was seized with remorse and returned the thirty silver coins to the chief priests and the elders. 'I have sinned,' he said, 'for I have betrayed innocent blood.' "* —Matthew 27:3-4

Godly sorrow, on the other hand, results in peace and not regret. True repentance is the deliberate **TURNING** of one's heart and the **CHANGING** of one's mind.

True repentance is TURNING from sin to God.

The Bible has a lot to say about repentance, and it is fair to assume that it is therefore a very important aspect of the Christian faith. **Repentance is a command to believers, not an option.** Our initial salvation experience is hinged on repentance, and our daily walk with Christ depends on it as well. The New Testament reveals the aspect of repentance that deals with changing one's mind. It's important to understand that this is not an emotion, but a **CHOICE**. The Old Testament speaks of repentance more in the light of **turning**, or **returning**. And together we find the facets complementing one another: **Repentance is an inner change of mind resulting in an outward turning *(moving completely in a new direction)*.**

In Luke 15:11-32, Jesus tells the parable of the Prodigal Son in which an undeserving and greedy son squanders his father's fortune and comes to the end of himself in a foreign land. We are told that the son *"came to his senses"* and *"got up and went to his father"* with nothing but a broken will and a confession of his dependency. It is a model of true repentance, for the son experienced a change of heart, and he responded by turning back to his father.

The Foundation Stones
Repentance from Dead Works

There is another very important point to make about repentance, which leads us back to our dependence on God:

Repentance is a gift from God.

The Bible speaks about instructing those who oppose the Word of God *"in the hope that God will grant them repentance leading them to a knowledge of the truth"* (2 Timothy 2:25). Once again, we come to the place where God is asking something of us that only HE can give. It is no wonder that we struggle so much in our Christian walk; we are trying to play the game without knowing the rules. No matter how fast we run, we will never win the race if we are going in the wrong direction.

It is difficult to come to grips with what God desires of us. We live in a world where performance is the game, and we assume that God expects no less. Take, for instance, King David. Have you ever pondered the fact that David—the adulterer, schemer, and murderer—was also called "a man after God's own heart"? Does that not strike you as odd in the light of the accounts of others who were struck dead for less serious offenses? It leads us to one of two conclusions: either God wavers in His standards, **OR** we do not really understand what those standards are.

In 2 Samuel 12, we find an account of Nathan the prophet confronting and rebuking King David for the crimes he committed. David was not a perfect man by anybody's estimation (and especially not God's). God knew the evil that was in David's heart, just as He knows the evil that is in ours. God expects nothing more from our sinful nature. But the important thing to realize is that David was quick to TURN back to God. He did not hide his sin or make excuses. And he did not promise to do better the next time. He simply turned and threw himself on God's mercy and grace. Psalm 51 records David's response to God, a wonderful expression of repentance:

> *"Have mercy on me, O God, according to your unfailing love; according to your great compassion blot out my transgressions ... For I know my transgressions, and my sin is always before me. Against you, you only, have I sinned and done what is evil in your sight; so you are right in your verdict and justified when you judge ... Create in me a pure heart, O God, and renew a steadfast spirit within me. Do not cast me from your presence or take your Holy Spirit from me. Restore to me the joy of your salvation and grant me a willing spirit, to sustain me ... My sacrifice, O God, is a broken spirit; a broken and contrite heart you, God, will not despise."*
>
> —Psalm 51

David was fully aware of his condition apart from God, but he also knew very well the unconditional love that his Father had for him. And that's what caused him to run back each time he fell, and that is the only thing that will cause us to do the same. This is what made David "a man after God's own heart."

In contrast, it is interesting to read the account of King Saul, David's predecessor, who was rejected by God after becoming King. In 1 Samuel 15, we read about a similar confrontation between the prophet Samuel and King Saul, who had disobeyed God by neglecting to completely destroy the Amalekites. It seemed a minor offense compared to adultery, murder and the like, and so we expect God's mercy to be extended here as well. But there was a big difference in the condition of Saul's heart, and it is clearly seen in his response. He argues his innocence (1 Samuel 15:20), blames his soldiers (1 Samuel 15:21), and tries to cover his sin before the people (1 Samuel 15:24-25). He did not have a repentant heart, and that is all that God was concerned with. That is still all that God is concerned with today.

The Foundation Stones
Repentance from Dead Works

WHAT IS THE RESULT OF REPENTANCE?

John the Baptist, the cousin of Jesus, was also the prophet who ushered in the ministry of Jesus on this earth. His message, in short, was: *"Repent and believe the good news"* (Mark 1:15). In this verse, we find a God-given order. First, we are to **repent** (turn from sin to God), and then we can walk in **faith**. In Matthew 3:1-12, we find John the Baptist warning the Pharisees and Sadducees about their unrepentant hearts. In verse 10, He ties their condition in with lack of fruitfulness in God's Kingdom and warns: *"The ax is already at the root of the trees, and every tree that does not produce good fruit will be cut down and thrown into the fire."*

Repentance can be seen as the doorway to all that God has for His children —faith, fruitfulness, and true life. The door is always open and right before us at the level of our shame and guilt. But we must choose to go through it on a daily basis. Repentance, when it is cast aside, will be the very thing that separates us from God and robs us of faith. But it is the key to His boundless grace and mercy when it is embraced.

Jesus told His disciples that the Holy Spirit would be sent in order to lead us to repentance:

> *"When he comes, he will prove the world to be in the wrong about sin and righteousness and judgment: about sin, because people do not believe in me; about righteousness, because I am going to the Father, where you can see me no longer; and about judgment, because the prince of this world now stands condemned."*
>
> —John 16:7-11

Be sensitive to what the Holy Spirit is pointing to in your life. It is likely an area of independence from God, something from which you have not repented. It will bring your faith to a standstill until it is dealt with. The Holy Spirit's work is to open our eyes to sin, cause us to hunger for righteousness, and recognize God's judgment of all that is independent of Him.

Let us end on a very simple note: Let us listen to simple words; our Lord speaks simply: "Trust me, My child," He says. "Trust Me with a humbler heart and fuller abandon to My will than ever thou didst before. Trust Me to pour my love through thee, as minute succeeds minute. And if thou shouldst be conscious of anything hindering the flow, do not hurt My love by going away from Me in discouragement, for nothing can hurt love so much as that. Draw all the closer to Me; come, flee unto Me to hide thee, even from thyself. Tell Me about the trouble. Trust Me to turn My hand upon thee and thoroughly to remove the boulder that has choked thy riverbed, and take away all the sand that has silted up the channel. I will not leave thee until I have done that which I have spoken to thee of. I will perfect that which concerneth thee. Fear thou not, O child of My love; fear not."

— author unknown

NOTES:

The Foundation Stones
Repentance from Dead Works

AUTHORITY

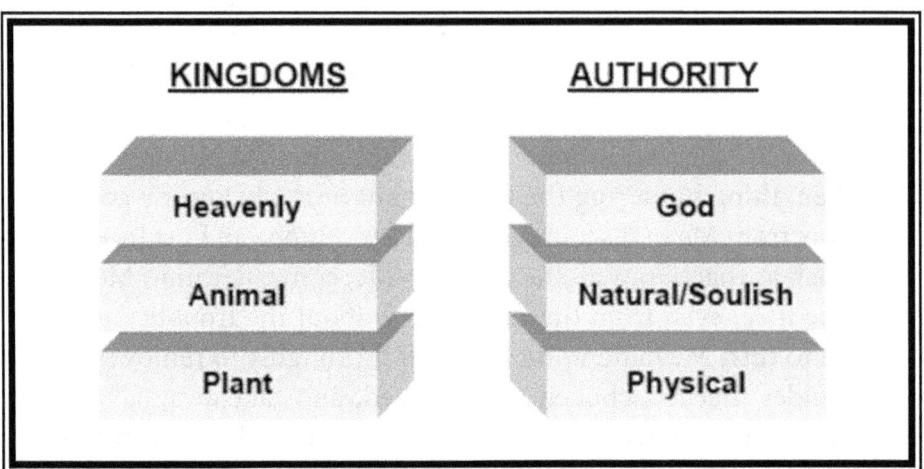

Repentance is not an isolated activity, as we are beginning to see. It directly affects our walk with Christ and our ability to experience His life. Now we want to talk about a different aspect of repentance, which deals with the authority God has established on this earth. The three-tiered hierarchies shown above are closely related, for in each kingdom there exists a corresponding authority. Let's look at each level more closely so that we might understand how they work together, as well as their relevance to the matter of repentance.

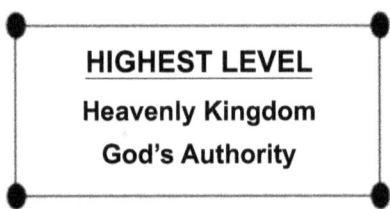

The **Heavenly Kingdom** is just as real as the others, but it must be spiritually discerned. Humans cannot physically see God, the Holy Spirit, or the spiritual forces of darkness. That is why, as believers, we are called to walk by faith and not by sight. When we choose to turn to God in repentance and brokenness, we are essentially submitting to **God's authority** in response to the Holy Spirit within us.

Repentance, in this light, is the act of turning to God as the authority over our feelings, emotions, and reasoning. We as humans can be deceived in any and every part of our souls—mind, emotions, and will. **But God cannot**.

We are instructed in Luke 10:27 to *"Love the Lord your God with all your heart and with all your soul and with all your strength and with all your mind."*

In other words, we are called to submit all that is within us to the loving authority of our Father. We must choose to refer to and depend on God over all other things. True repentance and submission brings us under Spiritual authority, authority that protects and guards us. And it is here that we are TRANSFORMED into His image. Not only was this God's original plan for His creation, but it is the heritage of His children today as well.

MIDDLE LEVEL

Animal Kingdom

Natural/Soulish Authority

The Animal Kingdom is governed by the law known to us as "Survival of the Fittest." As animals in the wild continually fend for a higher position in their circles, so do humans in a sense. When we fail to operate inside the parameters of the Heavenly Kingdom and God's Authority, we default to a survival mode in which our own needs are the driving force behind all we do. **Natural** or **Soulish Authority** refers to the governing laws and the actual agents of law-enforcement that are established on this earth to keep order.

Chapter 13 of Romans talks about submission to the authorities, and it gives us an interesting perspective on the sovereignty of God even in secular arenas. *"Let everyone be subject to the governing authorities, for there is no authority except that which God has established. The authorities that exist have been established by God"* (Romans 13:1).

The Foundation Stones
Repentance from Dead Works

Lack of repentance brings us under this **Natural Authority** because we are no longer referring to God. Instead, we put ourselves under the Law and, through behavior modification, are CONFORMED to the world system.

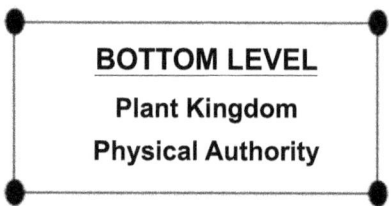

The **Plant Kingdom**—the lowest of the three—also tends to be the most dominant in today's world. Consider the substances we produce from plants: food, drugs, tobacco, and alcohol. The control that these four things have over humans as a whole is astounding. And those who struggle with addictions to any degree have fallen from the divine purposes of God to become slaves to physical gratification.

When humans aspire to nothing more than to *"gratify the desires of the flesh"* (Galatians 5:16), then **God's authority** and **Natural Authority** are not enough. **Physical Authority** is most clearly illustrated in prisons. Here we find men and women who have thrown off the constraints of the law (not to mention repentance) and have resorted to acts of violence and/or deceit to gratify their sinful desires. Their human rights are taken away, and they are controlled by physical restraints and punishment.

With these illustrations, we can see how these three Kingdoms and these levels of Authority exist even within ourselves. First Thessalonians 5:23 reads, *"May God Himself, the God of peace, sanctify you through and through. May your whole spirit, soul, and body be kept blameless at the coming of our Lord Jesus Christ."*

In this verse Paul explains that we are made up of **spirit**, **soul**, and **body**. And it is easy to see how the dominance of one part over the others will influence our choice of authority. If we choose to be led by the Holy Spirit and repent, then we are submitting to God, the highest authority. If, on the other hand, we follow our sinful desires, whether soulish or physical, then we are putting ourselves under the Law, or physical authority. But take note of one important thing: We are **all** under some kind of authority. We are **all** servants to whomever or whatever we submit to. The verse below speaks to how we can honor God with all that is within us:

> *"Therefore, I urge you, brothers and sisters, in view of God's mercy, to offer your bodies as a living sacrifice, holy and pleasing to God— this is your true and proper worship. Do not conform to the pattern of this world, but be transformed by the renewing of your mind."*
> —Romans 12:1-2

THE REPENTANT HEART

Let's take a closer look at the truly repentant heart. We have already talked about King David, who was called "a man after God's own heart" (see Acts 13:22). And we have come to the conclusion that David was far from perfect but sincere in repentance. In Psalm 51:17 (NKJV) David wrote, *"The sacrifices of God are a broken spirit, a **broken** and a **contrite** heart— these, O God, You will not despise."* Do you think David knew something that we often miss? He knew what God desired of him, even in the aftermath of his sin.

Read through the following verses paying special attention to the attributes God is looking for in His children:

> *"The Lord is near to those who have a broken heart, and saves such as have a contrite spirit."* —Psalm 34:18 (NKJV)

> *"These are the ones I look on with favor: those who are humble and contrite in spirit, and who tremble at my word."* —Isaiah 66:2

The Foundation Stones
Repentance from Dead Works

All three of these heart attributes—**broken**, **contrite**, and **humble**—point to repentance. When we are painfully aware of our condition apart from God, our hearts will be broken, we will feel deeply sorry for our sins (contrite), and we will be humble before the God who washes us clean of all unrighteousness. When we can live in the light of these truths, understanding the ramifications of them more each day, then our hearts will be pleasing to God.

Philippians 2:1-11 calls us to be imitators of Christ's humility. It tells us that Christ (the Son of God, keep in mind) *"made himself nothing by taking the very nature of a servant"* (v.7). And in verse 3, we are told to *"Do nothing out of selfish ambition or vain conceit. Rather, in humility value others above yourselves."*

We can also look to Luke 22:26-27 that records the disciples arguing about which of them was the greatest. Jesus, to their dismay, tells them, *"[T]he greatest among you should be like the youngest, and the one who rules like the one who serves ... I am among you as one who serves."*

So we have been shown by the example of Jesus that our humility is to overflow into the lives of others in the form of serving. The repentant heart is the heart that God hears and can work through for His own purposes.

> *"[I]f my people, who are called by my name, will humble themselves and pray and seek my face and turn from their wicked ways, then I will hear from heaven, and I will forgive their sin and will heal their land."* —2 Chronicles 7:14

Stop a minute to think about the following questions and the underlying purpose of all that we do as the Church of Jesus Christ.

> What would be the purpose of **MISSIONS** if our hearts
> were not broken to serve?
>
> • • •
>
> What would be the purpose of **EVANGELISM** if we
> were not able to lead by the Spirit?
>
> • • •
>
> What would be the purpose of simple **FELLOWSHIP** if we
> were not obedient to release God's love?

What we need is not more **teaching** but more **EXPERIENCE** of God. Romans 5:17 tells us that we are to *"reign in life"* by receiving *"God's abundant provision of grace and of the gift of righteousness."*

> ## LET'S ALL ASK OURSELVES:
>
> **Are we reigning?**
>
> • • •
>
> **Are we receiving God's abundant provision of grace?**
>
> • • •
>
> **Do we even see our need for it?**

The Foundation Stones
Repentance from Dead Works

THE ROOT OF DEAD WORKS

So far we have talked about **sin** (living independently of God) and **repentance** (turning from sin and to God), and we have also touched on the subject of **dead works** (those produced independent of God). But you may still be wondering why the focus of this foundation stone is repentance from *dead works* and not from *sin*. In order to answer this question, we must go back to the beginning, that is, the VERY beginning.

ADAM and EVE

In Genesis Chapter 2, we find the short account of the life of Adam and Eve before "The Fall." We are told that they walked in unhindered communion with God, the fruit of which was security, peace, love, and acceptance. In short, they enjoyed abundant LIFE from the Source of Life Himself. But, as we all know, it was not long before the pair gravitated to the single forbidden tree in the garden and found themselves separated from God and cast out of paradise.

It is a frustrating story, to say the least, and especially when we realize that our own sinful nature is the result of Adam and Eve's deception. But do not be so quick to pass judgment on them. You may be surprised to find that you and I have eaten of the same tree most of our lives. The Bible gives no indication that this account is merely figurative, so we are left to assume that these events actually did occur. However, there are also some very important principles set forth by this story, and we would do well to understand them. After all, this is where the whole thing started.

> *"In the middle of the garden were the **tree of life** and the **tree of the knowledge of good and evil** ... And the Lord God commanded the man, 'You are free to eat from any tree in the garden; but you must not eat from the tree of the knowledge of good and evil, for when you eat from it, you will surely die.'"*
>
> —Genesis 2:9-17 (emphasis added)

The Foundation Stones
Repentance from Dead Works

Have you ever wondered why the tree of the knowledge of good and evil was so bad? Did God really want Adam and Eve to be ignorant of good and evil? And how did their disobedience result in death? This is what we are about to find out.

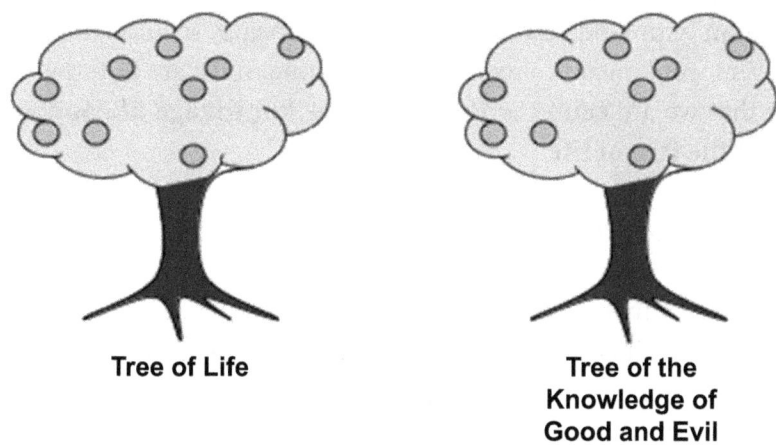

Tree of Life

Tree of the Knowledge of Good and Evil

When Satan tempted Eve to eat the forbidden fruit, his promise to her was, *"[Y]our eyes will be opened, and you will be like God, knowing good and evil"* (Genesis 3:5). It seems like a worthy endeavor at first glance, but there is a big catch. You see, God did not mean for us to *know evil*. Nor were we meant to *know good* **apart from Him**. This is the deception of the human race. If we consider ourselves good, moral people, then we probably do not struggle with temptations to DO EVIL (murder, stealing, etc.). BUT, we are continually trying to DO GOOD that is from the **same root** (not generated by God). The tree of the knowledge of good and evil is bad because the ROOT is not of God. Whether we are doing evil apart from God or doing good apart from God, WE ARE STILL LIVING INDEPENDENTLY OF GOD (sin).

Before this happened, the only good that Adam and Eve knew was God Himself. And it was not mere knowledge but a daily experience. They were essentially living off the **Tree of Life**, being sustained by the Life-Giver. But the moment they exchanged mere knowledge of good for the real thing (for *true good* comes only from God), they began to die spiritually. We see evidence of this death immediately in their reactions. They were **afraid**,

The Foundation Stones
Repentance from Dead Works

they felt **shame**, and they **hid** from God (see Genesis 3:7-10). Have you ever been in this very spot? Haven't we all?

Romans 7:4 tells us that we are in intimate relationship with Jesus *"in order that we might bear fruit for God."* (See also Colossians 1:6.) Just as Adam's communion with God resulted in the fruit of peace, security, love, etc., we as believers were meant to experience the same. If we are not, then we can be sure that we are eating of **the tree of the knowledge of good and evil** instead of **the tree of life.**

You may still wonder where the **death** comes in. Romans 6:23 very plainly tells us that *"the wages of sin is death."* And we are told in Ephesians 2:1 and Colossians 2:13 that *"you were dead in your transgressions and sins"* apart from the Life of Christ. You see, **GOD IS LIFE**, and separation from God is death. In this state, we can only produce **dead works**, works apart from God (birthed from the tree of the knowledge of good and evil).

We all have inherited Adam's sin. We think we can find goodness in ourselves, but the truth is that our best efforts are **DEAD WORKS** in God's eyes because they come from a dead source. Those who do not have LIFE—that which is found in an intimate relationship with their Creator—are only alive in the biological sense. They CANNOT please God. And we, as believers, will never please God either until we repent (turn) from our dead works and receive His life.

It is important to pay attention to God's response to the "Original Sin" because it gives us a better understanding of how He deals with us.

> *"But the Lord God called to the man, 'Where are you?'"*
> —Genesis 3:9

It seems like a silly question coming from the Omnipresent God. Of course, He knew where Adam was hiding. He was really asking, "Where are you in relationship with Me?" God came to Adam immediately in His mercy to

The Foundation Stones
Repentance from Dead Works

make him aware of his separation from Life. And He comes to us in the same way whenever we are hiding in our sin.

The Bible tells us that we are reconciled to the same choice that Adam and Eve had by the blood of Jesus. We are indeed born into sin and death, but we have been given the privilege to receive God's Life instead. It is our natural tendency to embrace fear, anxiety, anger, condemnation, guilt, pride, etc. *(all from the tree of the knowledge of good and evil)*. The moment we do, however, we begin to experience death, separation from God.

> *"You must not eat fruit from the tree that is in the middle of the garden, and you must not touch it, or you will die."* —Genesis 3:3

It is our choice moment by moment. We must consciously repent and go to the **Tree of Life** if we are to experience Life.

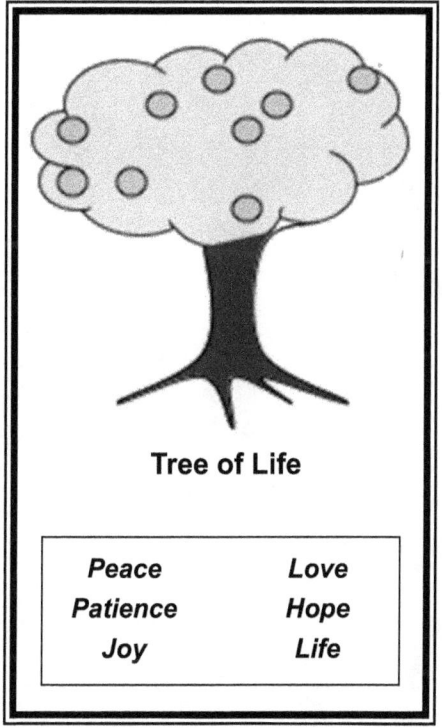

Tree of Life

Peace	Love
Patience	Hope
Joy	Life

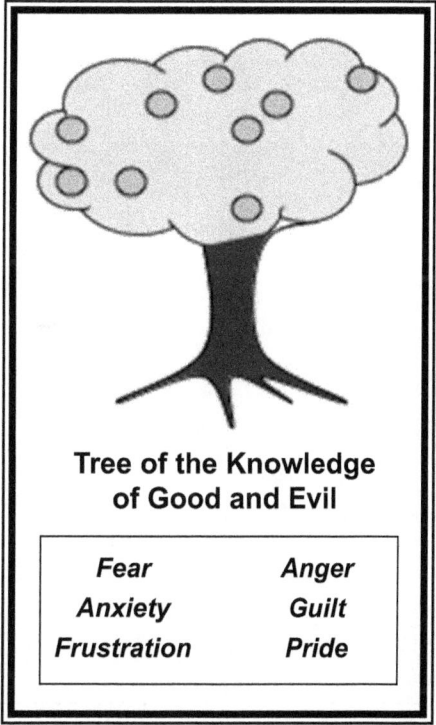

Tree of the Knowledge of Good and Evil

Fear	Anger
Anxiety	Guilt
Frustration	Pride

The Foundation Stones
Repentance from Dead Works

The important thing to remember is that REPENTANCE takes us on a path that is not always logical in our own eyes. We are instructed to do things that go against our nature, the traditions of the world, and often our own desires. Remember the Sovereign God Who has called you to walk the Path of Life, and put your trust in Him over your mind, emotions, and will.

"There is a way that seems right to a man, but its end is the way of death." —Proverbs 14:12 NKJV

Do we need any more of a reason to abandon our own devices? They are always going to lead us away from God.

NOTES:

The Foundation Stones
Repentance from Dead Works

RIGHTEOUSNESS AND DEAD WORKS

The term "**righteousness,**" as it is used in the Bible, can be defined as **a right standing with God**. And the Scriptures have a lot to say about the subject. After all, this very thing has been the motivation behind every religious endeavor in history. Deep inside each human is an unquenchable desire to be right with God, and yet our sinful nature seems to be the ever-present barrier. Have you ever struggled with the notion of standing—exposed of your sin—before a Holy God? This is the vexing predicament of the entire human race. We are born into the sinful condition that separates us from God and, even after we've been saved, we often choose to believe that we are still unacceptable. But God's answer to our sin through Jesus Christ has already been given, and it is crucial that we understand it well.

In Scripture, there are TWO types of righteousness identified—**God's** and **our own**. And these coincide with the two trees in the Garden of Eden that we learned about in the previous lesson.

The **Tree of Life**, in essence, represents **God's righteousness**, which is a gift of God and must be received by faith. The **tree of the knowledge of good and evil**, on the other hand, stands for **self-righteousness**. If we are not walking by faith in the provision of God, then we can be sure that we are seeking a righteousness of our own through works. They are not only completely different, but they are diametrically opposed. In fact, they are at war with one another for our allegiance each and every day. Let's take a closer look at God's righteousness.

The Foundation Stones
Repentance from Dead Works

GOD'S RIGHTEOUSNESS ...

Is not of ourselves but from God.

"*[N]ot having a righteousness of my own that comes from the law, but that which is through faith in Christ—the righteousness that comes from God on the basis of faith.*" —Philippians 3:9 (see also: Ephesians 2:8)

Is not through works but by faith.

"*For in the gospel the righteousness of God is revealed—a righteousness that is by faith from first to last, just as it is written: 'The righteous will live by faith.'*" —Romans 1:17 (see also: Ephesians 2:8-9, Galatians 2:16, 3:6, 3:11, Romans 3:20-22, 9:31-32, 4:13, 1:17)

Is not earned but a gift.

"*[T]hose who receive God's abundant provision of grace and of the gift of righteousness reign in life through the one man, Jesus Christ!*" —Romans 5:17

Is not merited but an act of mercy.

"*He saved us, not because of righteous things we had done, but because of his mercy.*" —Titus 3:5

Is not merely given to us but created in us.

"*God made him who had no sin to be sin for us, so that in him we might become the righteousness of God.*" —2 Corinthians 5:21 (see also: Romans 5:19 and Isaiah 54:14)

The Foundation Stones
Repentance from Dead Works

What do you suppose is the true cause of our self-righteous tendency? Maybe pride, self-centeredness, or rebellion? Maybe. But perhaps we are overlooking the core of the problem altogether. For it seems only logical that we would RUN to the mercy of God that is extended to us, and especially in the light of our sinful condition. Why do we turn away instead?

The next time you read through Genesis, pay attention to the deception of the "Original Sin." What was Satan's main objective when he tempted Eve? It was to DISTORT HER VIEW OF GOD. When she began to doubt God's heart for her, she was quick to turn away from Him. In the same way we are confronted with lies about our Father every day, and most of us do not even recognize them. What has Satan convinced YOU of regarding God's heart toward you? If you feel condemned, ashamed, or inadequate in His presence, you have believed a lie. And that false perception is what drives you to seek out your own righteousness—hoping that someday you will be good enough to be accepted by Him.

> Our ambition to *do for God* is often motivated by our desire to be accepted by Him—when *WE ALREADY ARE.*

God's unconditional acceptance is ours right now. But it is only ours if we receive it as the free gift that it is. It is when we strive to EARN it that we end up with dead works.

> *"Since they did not know the righteousness of God and sought to establish their own, they did not submit to God's righteousness."*
> —Romans 10:3

This verse refers to those who refuse to **believe, submit to,** and be **credited with** God's righteousness and instead **seek to establish their own.** Why, according to this verse, do people pursue self-righteousness? BECAUSE

The Foundation Stones
Repentance from Dead Works

THEY DO NOT **KNOW** THE RIGHTEOUSNESS THAT COMES FROM GOD. They do not **know** who they are in God's eyes, nor do they understand God's heart for them. Simple **ignorance** of God's righteousness always leads to "religion," which means conforming to laws and regulations **instead** of responding to God's love.

> *"For Christ is the **end** of the law for righteousness to everyone who believes."* —Romans 10:4 (NKJV) (emphasis added)

The word "**end**" in this verse is defined as *that which completes a thing or renders it perfect.* Paul is essentially saying that, on the cross, Christ has accomplished the purpose for which the law was given. And there can be nothing taken away from or added to that finished work, especially not any action on our part other than to believe. And what is the purpose of it all? It has been done in order that the righteousness of God may be bestowed upon everyone "**WHO BELIEVES.**" We are not saved by works, and there will never be a point at which God's grace ends and we must pick up.

Christ has not only **made** the way, but we are told in the book of John that He **IS** that way. Christ is the ONLY way to everything we will ever need.

> *"Jesus answered, 'I am the way and the truth and the life. No one comes to the Father except through me.'"* — John 14:6

Immediately following the account of Adam and Eve, we find another tragic story (see Genesis 4:1-8). This time it concerns **Cain** and **Abel**, their sons. In short, God required a particular type of offering from the brothers. Abel complied fully, but Cain chose to take a different approach—his own. God blatantly rejected Cain's offering, but Abel found favor in God's eyes. The anger and jealousy that resulted led to the first murder recorded in the Bible.

You are likely familiar with the story already and have probably wondered why God responded to Cain's good intentions so harshly. After all, he was trying to please God, wasn't he? What do you think, is God really that strict when it comes to how we serve Him? The offering of fruit instead of livestock may not strike you as the worst of transgressions, but choosing our own ways over God's ways certainly is. It may have seemed good and honorable to Cain, but what was the source of it? SELF-RIGHTEOUSNESS! Consider again this proverb:

> *"There is a way that seems right to a man, but in the end it leads to death."* —Proverbs 14:12

Does God likewise reject our dead works so that He can teach us to walk in Life? We had better hope so. For without the light of truth shining in our hearts, we will most certainly be deceived. The bigger question is, will we respond with a willing heart? We can easily frustrate the grace of God if we do not.

> *"[K]now that a man is not justified by the works of the law but by faith in Jesus Christ ... by the works of the law no flesh shall be justified ... I do not set aside the grace of God; for if righteousness comes through the law, then Christ died in vain."*
> —Galatians 2:16-21 (NKJV)

When Jesus walked this earth, which group of people did He rebuke most severely? It was not the *sinful* prostitutes, drunkards, or tax collectors. They were actually drawn to Him and were receptive of His mercy. It was the **RELIGIOUS PEOPLE** of the day that Jesus opposed. Have you ever wondered why that was? These were the people that the verse above addresses. They had set aside the grace of God and were trying to gain righteousness through the law. They had rejected Christ's work and were leading others to do the same. Jesus told them,

> *"You study the Scriptures diligently because you think that in them you have eternal life. These are the very Scriptures that testify about me, yet you refuse to come to me to have life."* —John 5:39-40

The Foundation Stones
Repentance from Dead Works

Would Jesus' response be any different to the religious people of today? Sometimes we think the answers we are searching for will be found in more **knowledge** of the Bible. But the fact is that, even if we memorize the Bible from cover to cover, we will someday find ourselves eternally separated from God if we do not have a relationship with Him.

The truth of the matter is this: God did not create you and me to WORK for Him, but for a RELATIONSHIP! We must come empty-handed to God, seeking only to understand His love for us. Turn the fire of first love to God and not to working. God writes His law on the hearts of believers, and good works will spring forth as the RESULT (not the cause) of our righteousness in Him.

The Bible tells us that God sees only the righteousness of Jesus when He looks at His children. Imagine that. To Him, it is as if we have never sinned at all! Hebrews 9:14 tells us that the blood of Christ will "cleanse our consciences from acts that lead to death" (dead works, as we have been calling them). His work in us is complete, EVEN IF IT DOES NOT FEEL LIKE IT! If we struggle with these things, it is simply because we have believed a lie, about ourselves and about God.

> "[T]hat the sharing of your faith may become effective by the acknowledgement of every good thing which is in you in Christ Jesus."
> —Philemon 6 (NKJV)

This verse tells us that when we choose to believe what God has said about us (apart from how we feel or what we see), our faith becomes **effective.** And it is here that God's creative power begins to work in our hearts to bring these very things to pass in you and me. But remember that it is YOUR CHOICE that God is waiting on.

You Are What You Think

Essentially, we tend to be shaped by what our minds think about most often. If you always think about yourself, you'll probably become an egotist. If you think about material things all the time, you'll most likely become materialistic. If you dwell on your fears, doubtless you'll grow paranoid; if on others' wrongs, you'll become bitter. But imagine, just imagine, what would happen if your thoughts focused not on bitterness but on the forgiveness of Christ … not on your fears but on the hope you have in Christ … not on selfish accumulation of things but on the unselfishness of the Savior … not on exalted thoughts of yourself but on His lowliness. May I lift the shade of your personal thoughts and take a peek? What clutters your cranium? Work? Worries? Why not have a garage sale and get rid of some of that junk, and rearrange your mental furniture around Jesus?   (Hebrews 12:1-3)

—unknown author

The Foundation Stones
Repentance from Dead Works

BELIEVING THE TRUTH

We have explored the connection between dead works and self-righteousness, and we have also learned that self-righteousness is the result of ignorance, that is, ignorance of the truth. Maybe you have come to the conclusion that you have indeed believed lies about yourself and about God. If your core beliefs don't line up with what the Bible tells us, then this is the case. Where do we go from here? Obviously, fixing the **symptoms** of deception will not accomplish the goal. We have to go back to the SOURCE. Before we go any further, we need to answer three very important questions:

Why Does God Love Me?

Who Am I?

What Is My Purpose In Life?

The questions seem simple enough, but you may be surprised by how difficult they are to answer. Take a moment to think about and write down your thoughts before we continue. This will give us a good indication of how well we understand our identity in Christ.

Why does God love me?

_____

_____

Who am I?

_____

_____

What is my purpose in life?

_____

_____

Why does God love me?
Because He created me!

Think about it for a minute. Why do you love your own children? Is it because of the way they look or the things they do? Is it because they love you back? Consider a newborn baby. It goes without saying that a newborn has absolutely nothing to offer his parents. He cannot understand them, obey them, or even return their affection. What has he done to merit their love? Absolutely nothing. You love your children because they are yours, and they are, in a sense, created in your image. How are we any different from this in God's eyes? God created you and me in His own image and breathed life into us. The Bible tells us that He knew us, and loved us, before we were ever conceived. His love is unconditional. **God loves me because He created me.** PERIOD!

Who am I?
I am a child of the King!

Imagine yourself the child of an earthly king. You are born into a wealthy, affluent, and ROYAL family, no less. You do not **deserve** the rights and privileges you have inherited any more than the son of a pauper deserves the lack of them. But, regardless, they are bestowed upon you in fullness. There is nothing you will lack because there is no limit to the resources of a king. You can stand tall and confident because the king's child is WHO YOU ARE and not something you must live up to or earn. And, thus, your identity can never be taken away from you.

But let's say that you are separated from your father at birth, and you grow up on the streets. Alongside the paupers, you beg for bread and struggle to survive each day. When your father eventually finds you, you refuse to believe that you are anything more than an orphan and decide that you could never give up your familiar life even if it were true. If you live out the rest of your days on the streets, never believing that you are a child of the king, does that change the fact that you are a child of the king? Do the rags and dirt nullify your royal blood?

The Foundation Stones
Repentance from Dead Works

Now imagine a child of the KING OF KINGS, the CREATOR of everything choosing to live in spiritual poverty. God's riches are ours in abundance, and our inheritance is secure in Him. We are eternally His by grace alone. If we are living as paupers, it is because we have refused to believe that we are who God says we are. But just as the value of a $20 bill does not diminish with age or wear, nothing we do or experience can change our worth in God's eyes.

What is my purpose in life?
I was created for a relationship with God!

Most of us, in answer to this question, would probably say, "I was created to serve God." Do you realize that all of nature **serves** God. Even Satan serves the purposes of God. Sometimes it seems that our highest goal is to be **used by** Him. But is that really what we desire?

What do you see as the purpose for your marriage? Is it to be **used by** your husband or wife? It sounds silly, but is it any more so than saying this about God? He created us for His good pleasure, and our purpose is to know Him and to walk with Him in intimate relationship. In Mark 3:13, it says that *"Jesus went up on a mountainside and called to him those he **wanted**."* God can USE **anybody**, even the most ungodly of persons, to accomplish His will. Remember that our "usefulness" to God is in **His** hands. I don't know about you, but I would much rather be **wanted** by Him. And that is what we, His children, are.

THE SOURCE

Now that we have likely exposed some areas of unbelief or ignorance in our own lives, we need to discuss how these lies affect us and what we must do in order to replace them with the truth. But just in case you are still skeptical about the seriousness of your condition apart from God's intervention, read the verses on the next page. Keep in mind that these speak to **all** people, both those who are His children and those who are not. For without God's saving grace, we are all hopeless.

The Foundation Stones
Repentance from Dead Works

"Surely the arm of the Lord is not too short to save, nor his ear too dull to hear. But your iniquities have separated you from your God; your sins have hidden his face from you, so that he will not hear. For your hands are stained with blood, your fingers with guilt."
—Isaiah 59:1-8

"What shall we conclude then? Do we have any advantage? Not at all! We have already made the charge that Jews and Gentiles alike are all under the power of sin. As it is written: 'There is no one righteous, not even one; there is no one who understands; there is no one who seeks God.'" —Romans 3:9-23

"The Lord looks down from heaven on all mankind to see if there are any who understand, any who seek God. All have turned away, all have become corrupt; there is no one who does good, not even one."
—Psalm 14:2-3

What do you suppose has brought the human race to such a condition as descibed in the previous verses? How is it that we have ALL in one accord turned from what is good? Let's revert once again to Adam's relationship with God, both before and after "The Fall." For it is at this point in history that the chasm between God and mankind was formed.

In the beginning, Adam's world revolved around God. Everything Adam KNEW to be true, THOUGHT about, BELIEVED in, and LIVED stemmed from his relationship with his Creator. GOD WAS HIS SOURCE. We have used the word "source" several times already in this section. Generally speaking, a source is the beginning and motivation behind everything that follows from it. Suppose, for instance, that we are writing a research paper on a particular subject. We find a single book in the library from which to glean information. If this book is our only source, then our understanding of the subject will likely reflect the opinion of the author, and the paper itself will be limited to the parameters of the book. In other words, we can rationally assume that our research paper will not "rise above its source."

The Foundation Stones
Repentance from Dead Works

In the same way, our **spiritual source** will determine the level at which we function. Our source will be either **God** (the truth) or a **lie** of the enemy. You see, our own **sources** have already been tainted. Even from birth, our thoughts and beliefs have been preverted by the world around us, and we simply cannot trust them. If, in any area, we are not referring to God and walking in the truth, then we can be sure we are being motivated by a lie. We must continually check our source and choose to believe God over all else. That is the essence of repentance.

Do you remember the tree of the knowledge of good and evil? Guess what this tree became to Adam and Eve when they sinned: their SOURCE. They had exchanged Life for Death when they chose a source apart from God. And it is interesting to note that this simple change in source dramatically and INSTANTLY altered Adam and Eve's perception. For you see, if your source is not God, then God will not have a place in your **knowledge**, your **thinking**, your **beliefs**, or your **lifestyle** either. For they all flow from the same source. Look at the diagram below, and notice how the source affects all of these elements in turn.

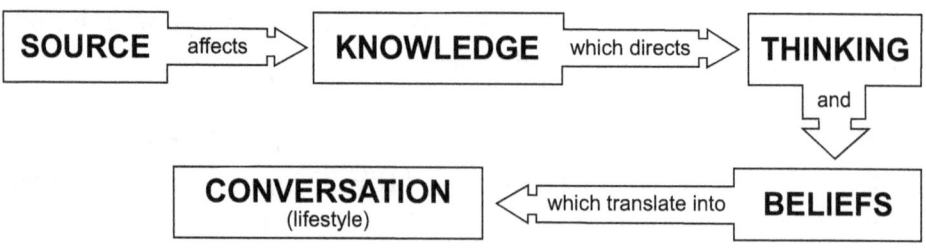

When Adam's source changed, his **knowledge** of God was immediately affected. Adam doubted God's heart and His ability to forgive, he began to **think** and **believe** that God was not able to meet his needs, and then he ran from God. You see, Adam's actions stemmed not from his experience of God (for God had shown Adam nothing but favor and goodness) but from his new ungodly source (the lies he believed).

Do you ever wonder why it is so hard to trust God even in light of His goodness towards you in the past? Have you recognized in yourself a tendency to hide from God in times of shame or fear? Pay close attention to your thoughts, your beliefs, your actions, and your knowledge of God. They will betray your source every time.

In Genesis 3:10, Adam says to God, *"I heard you in the garden, and I was afraid because I was naked; so I hid."* God's response to Adam? ***"Who told you that you were naked?"*** *(v.13)*. Why was God asking such a question (to which, of course, He already knew the answer)? HE WAS ENCOURAGING ADAM TO IDENTIFY HIS **SOURCE**. God knows that we do not intend to be deceived. That is the art of deception; it is blinding. We may not always be sure of the validity of a thought or belief, that is unless we identify the **source** of it. For we can be sure that anything that does not have God as its source (no matter how believable it seems) is a LIE.

STRONGHOLDS

Let's talk for a minute about lies, and particularly STRONGHOLDS. After all, these are the building blocks of any ungodly source.

A stronghold is a fortified lie.

It can be difficult to understand how someone who is a Christian can struggle with strongholds. The reasoning behind this, however, is actually very simple, for we are made up of three components: SPIRIT, SOUL, and BODY. When we are "born again," we are spiritually made alive. But there remains a struggle in our souls for dominion. We are "born again" once, but we must be SAVED every day—from ourselves, from sin, and from strongholds.

Our **souls** also consist of three elements—**Mind, Emotions,** and **Will**—and strongholds can exist in any or all of these areas. This means that the lies we believe can manifest in many different ways and affect people differently. Below are some examples:

Strongholds	Manifestations
MENTAL:	doubt, unbelief
EMOTIONAL:	fear, bitterness
WILLFUL:	passivity, irresponsibility

A stronghold, as we have said, is a **fortified lie**, meaning that it has been reinforced and built up throughout a period of time. When the enemy finds us susceptible to a particular lie (usually at a young age), he will concentrate his efforts in that area, hoping to render us useless for God's purposes. When we have a stronghold, we will filter everything that we see and hear through it. If it is a stronghold of doubt, then everything we perceive will be tainted with doubt. If we struggle with a stronghold of fear, then we can be sure that fear will be at every turn.

So we find that the power of a lie is in its ability to blind us to the truth. We CANNOT walk victoriously in Christ if we are deceived in any area, and so knowing and believing the truth is half the battle. But it is important to keep this in mind regarding lies:

> Believing a lie does not make it the truth.

It is common knowledge that believing something does not make it so. None of us, most likely, managed to escape this disappointment as children. We have long since learned that our imaginations never spill over into reality. But, unfortunately, the same principal becomes a little trickier when we are dealing with the lies of the enemy. Isn't it nice to know that you **are** who God says you are even if it does not seem that way? Be careful, however, that you do not stop there. It is one thing to **know** the truth, but **believing** it is entirely different. **For, to believe as the Bible calls us to believe, we must TRUST, RELY ON, and CLING TO the truth.** And this is where we are deceived most often. If we were to MEMORIZE the entire Word of God from cover to cover and yet fail to respond to it as the truth, we will prove that we really do not believe God. The sad reality is that many of us, by simply not believing, miss out on EVERYTHING that God has for us, for it can be received only through **faith** (choosing to believe) and not mere knowledge.

To make matters worse, the power of a lie is fueled by our responses to it. Have you ever been awakened in the middle of the night by a noise and faced the possibility that there was an intruder in your house? Of course, ninety-nine percent of the time there is not, but the thought alone can be enough to drive anyone mad. If you give it place in your mind, you will find that the house comes alive with noises to support the notion. Don't lies always work this way, like a giant snowball of evidence in our minds? When we choose to believe a lie, it begins to manifest in our lives. It will become our reality. We will **LIVE OUT** the lies we are believing.

If lies are so menacing, why do you think we are so reluctant to separate ourselves from them, even after they have been exposed? It is because we have believed all along that the bad habits, mood swings, temperment, critical spirit, etc., ARE WHO WE ARE! Over time, the lies we believe become intermingled in our personalities so that we recognize them as part of us. And so we protect them as we would protect ourselves, even from the truth. Too far-fetched to believe? Think about it. When was the last time you said something like, "That's just how I am," or "I've always been like that," or even "I've inherited [some trait] from my father/mother"? The truth is that anything in your personality that does not line up with the character of God is **NOT** WHO YOU ARE but a lie that you have embraced. Until we are willing to accept this, we will walk in deception.

The Foundation Stones
Repentance from Dead Works

THE GOOD NEWS?

You may wonder at this point, where do we go from here? If we are truly deceived to the extent that our personalities are tied up in strongholds, and if the lies blind us to the truth, how can we experience freedom? Once again, the answer lies in our **source**. If our lifestyles, habits, thoughts, and beliefs are wrong, it is because our source is wrong. And it is only in changing our source that we have any hope.

> *"Do not conform to the pattern of this world, but be transformed by the renewing of your mind."* —Romans 12:2a

In the verse above, we are told that the **renewing of our minds** will **TRANSFORM** us *(metamorphosis)*. Why do you think we must first separate ourselves from the thinking of this world and be renewed in our minds before we can be transformed? It is because we have believed lies, and our sources are tainted. Every chance we get, we must go back to God as our source, and He will transform us by His truth. The Bible tells us that, as we look to God, we are changed "from glory to glory" into His likeness (2 Corinthians 3:18 NKJV).

Lies can be intimidating because of the power they have in our lives. There is certainly good reason to be wary of their deceitfulness. But it is even more important to understand that we, as the children of the Almightly God, have no need to fear them. For the truth of God's Word possesses the power to transform, make new, and even CREATE what God speaks into our lives. So what do we do about the lies? We must simply recognize them for what they are—LIES—and treat them as such.

> *Consider for a moment the pneumatic (air-powered) tool. Without the power of compressed air, the tool is of no use to anyone. In the same way, we are all "empowered" by something, and being a Christian is not the issue. We have the opportunity to be empowered by the Spirit of God but only if we CHOOSE to make God our Source. The only alternative is deception.*

THE EFFECT OF RIGHTEOUSNESS

Any discussion about BELIEVING the truth will likely lead to the topic of **righteousness**. For we are told in God's Word that believing is credited to us as righteousness as it was in Abraham's case (see Genesis 15:6). And now we will talk about the effect that righteousness (believing the truth) has on our lives.

How often do you encounter Christians who are defeated, cast down, and hopeless? Most likely on a daily basis, for it seems to be the norm rather than the exception to the rule nowadays. How often do you recognize this very same pattern working in your own life?

We have strayed so far from God's purposes that most of us would not know true Christianity if it hit us in the nose. What we are very familiar with is RELIGION and the do's and don'ts of the Law, but a genuine Christian life is a far cry from the institutions of man. Was this not, after all, the very gap that confronted Jesus on this earth? The Pharisees, the Sadducees, and the Teachers of the Law never SAW Jesus for who He was because they were looking for an entirely different type of savior. Imagine that! MISSING the very thing they had been waiting hundreds of years for. Day in and day out, these men dwelt in the temple, studied the Scriptures, and speculated about the coming of their Savior, **and they missed it altogether**.

Amazing, isn't it? Yet, is it UNCOMMON? Do you suppose that we, the downtrodden Church, may be **missing** Jesus in our lives as well? Have we passed by the simplicity of Jesus' words with an "I already know that" in search of a deeply intellectual answer to our problems?

> "O thou afflicted, tossed with tempest, and not comforted"
> —Isaiah 54:11 (KJV)

The Foundation Stones
Repentance from Dead Works

This is God speaking to His children who were struggling with **oppression** *("afflicted")*, **fear** *("tossed with tempest")*, and **terror** *("not comforted")*. And if we read James Chapter One, we find that the cause of these things is simply UNBELIEF, which results in DOUBLE-MINDEDNESS. Look at the verse below:

> *"But when you ask, you must believe and not doubt, because the one who doubts is like a wave of the sea, blown and tossed by the wind. That person should not expect to receive anything from the Lord. Such a person is double-minded and unstable in all they do."*
> —James 1:5-8

Have you ever noticed how simple unbelief brings with it a truckload of other hindrances, such as fear, frustration, and unforgiveness? In the account of Jesus (and then Peter) walking on the water (Matthew 14:22-31), Jesus makes a clear connection between Peter's fear and his unbelief. And in 1 John 4:18, we are told that *"there is no fear in love"* and that *"perfect love drives out fear."* The things of Life and the things of Death seem to be mutually exclusive.

Then what, you may be wondering, is the effect that righteousness **should** have in our lives? Let's look at a couple more verses:

> *"if you continue in your faith, established and firm, and do not move from the hope held out in the gospel"* —Colossians 1:21-23

> *"rooted and built up in him, strengthened in the faith as you were taught, and overflowing with thankfulness."* —Colossians 2:7

> *"Surely the righteous will never be shaken; they will be remembered forever. They will have no fear of bad news; their hearts are steadfast, trusting in the Lord. Their hearts are secure, they will have no fear."*
> —Psalm 112:6-8

Are you starting to get the picture? Righteousness should have an effect on our lives that is exactly opposite the effect of unbelief. Instead of being tossed about, afflicted, and unstable, **righteousness causes our hearts to be steadfast, established, and secure.** Our lives should be overflowing with confidence, peace, trust, and thankfulness toward our Heavenly Father alone.

It all boils down to this: If we experience fear, unbelief, hopelessness, worry, tension, concern, depression, and the like in our day-to-day lives, then we are simply **not established in righteousness**.

Now, stop for a moment and consider the place in which you find yourself. What is our first instinct as humans when we see that we are lacking, even spiritually? When you fail to measure up to God's standards, what is your response? This is the point at which the path splits before us. For the Law was established to make us conscious of sin, to identify our separation from God. But what we DO with this revelation is up to us, and it is the determining factor in our walk with Christ.

Strangely enough, there is a certain appeal to RELIGION and even to the guidelines and restrictions that come with it. For we can appreciate and relate to an abiding-by-the-rules system much better than we can to faith and grace. To strive to earn our place with God is at least a tangible and noble endeavor, or so we think. And we have to admit that something within us really loathes the idea of lowering ourselves to the level of beggars —receiving without merit or effort. This path, religion, is certainly well-worn by travelers, and it is honorable in the eyes of men.

But consider that religion does not produce the righteousness that we are speaking of. The righteousness that causes us to be established and secure comes only from God's hand.

> *"The fruit of that righteousness will be peace; its effect will be quietness and confidence forever."* —Isaiah 32:17

The Foundation Stones
Repentance from Dead Works

Let's look at this verse for a minute. Why, when we are truly standing in the righteousness of God, will we experience peace, quietness, and confidence as the verse says? **It is because we are resting in the works of Jesus to be right with God instead of our own works.** It is the assurance that comes from knowing that God, and not my own strength, is keeping me. It is a wonderful place to be, understanding that I can do **nothing** to earn my place with God. Only the cross of Christ can give me a right standing with God, not what I have done today or will do tomorrow. Therefore, NOTHING can make me **UNRIGHTEOUS** (not even sin, the result of believing a lie), and NOTHING can make me **MORE RIGHTEOUS**! That is where true security comes from. Our only responsibility is to ABIDE (rest) in Him.

Too good to be true?   Too SIMPLE to work?

We, the children of God, do not have a "religion." Rules do not provide us with Salvation. We have a relationship with the living God, and we are sealed with His Holy Spirit. EFFORT has no part in this drama. Our only part is to **BELIEVE** and **RECEIVE** our righteousness in Christ.

NOTES:

The Foundation Stones
Repentance from Dead Works

THE DECEPTION OF RELIGION

It is because people throughout history have not understood God's ways that religion was instituted, and it is for that same reason that our culture today is comfortable with religion and not with God Himself. Whether you grew up in a religious setting or something far from it, you will likely be able to identify with the three areas of deception that are at the heart of religion (listed below). After all, religion is not the **cause** of our deception, but a **result** of it.

> The Abundance of God
>
> Our Freedom in Christ
>
> The Goodness of God

Satan has long been sowing seeds of deception into the hearts of people, Christian or otherwise. Let's return once again to the Garden of Eden, where we will see the pattern of deception as it was first executed, and as it still is.

In Genesis 2:16-17, God told Adam, *"You are free to eat from any tree in the garden; but you must not eat from the tree of the knowledge of good and evil, for when you eat from it you will surely die."* Shortly thereafter (in Chapter 3), we read Eve's conversation with the serpent regarding God's directions. It is in this brief exchange that deception enters into the heart of man in all three of the areas listed above. Let's take a closer look:

The Abundance of God

Notice firstly that the conversation between Eve and the serpent had a singular focus. The focus was on the ONE tree in the garden full of trees that was deemed **off-limits** by God. Eve quickly lost sight of God's abundant provision in light of what she DID NOT have and thought she needed.

The Foundation Stones
Repentance from Dead Works

How often we fall into the same trap. Most of us do not even realize that God has ALREADY given us an abundance. What do we have abundantly? The joy, peace, purpose, and hope that we plead to have from God **has already been given to us** through the blood of Christ. We pray the same prayers over and over again, prayers that God has answered long ago through His Son. It is our IGNORANCE of this fact that leads us to believe, just as Eve did, that God, in His silence, is **holding back** from us.

If we possess the abundance of God, then WHY do we not **experience** it? Good question. The problem is that the enemy has stolen our abundance, AND WE HAVE LET HIM DO IT. The book of Isaiah paints a picture of Satan's handiwork for us:

"By the strength of my hand I have done this, and by my wisdom, because I have understanding. I removed the boundaries of the nations, I plundered their treasures; like a mighty one I subdued their kings. As one reaches into a nest, so my hand reached for the wealth of the nations; as men gather abandoned eggs, so I gathered all the countries; not one flapped a wing, or opened its mouth to chirp."
—Isaiah 10:12-14

In this verse, we find the tactics of our spiritual enemy. The first thing Satan does is to **REMOVE OUR BOUNDARIES** so that we do not even know what is ours. If we do not know what belongs to us, we do not have much hope of defending it, do we? We could never even identify when the enemy was on "our land" without a right to be.

Second, Satan **ROBS OUR TREASURES** (joy, peace, etc.) so that we believe ourselves to be spiritually poor. And in case you have never noticed, poor people do not live and think as rich people do. Those who are poor often take on a **victim mentality**. They expect nothing good and often receive just that. If we truly believed that we are spiritually rich (as the Bible tells us we are), would we be hanging our heads and singing laments as we do?

Last, Satan **ROBS US OF GOD'S PROMISES**. Do you know that God's promises become ours as we hold onto them? Just as one would gather ABANDONED eggs, the enemy of our souls has robbed us. It is important to understand that **abandoned** eggs are hard to come by in everyday life. Animals defend their eggs with their very lives because they know that their eggs will bring forth life. And God's promises are no different—they produce LIFE in us if we hold on to them. We abandon them simply because we are **deceived**.

How many promises are you holding on to God for? We are told that Satan *"comes **only** to STEAL and KILL and DESTROY"* (John 10:10). Are you prepared? In Matthew 16:18, Jesus talks about prevailing against the "gates of Hell." Now, obviously, there would be no reason for us to storm the gates of Hell unless they surrounded something that belongs to us, our stolen goods in the spiritual sense. And all of these things can be restored to us just as quickly as they were stolen. HOW? **These things become mine once again WHEN I BELIEVE THEM!**

Let's get a better understanding of the ABUNDANCE that has been bestowed upon us:

> *"how much more will those who receive God's abundant provision of grace and of the gift of righteousness reign in life"*
> —Romans 5:17

> *"Blessed be the God and Father of our Lord Jesus Christ, who according to His abundant mercy has begotten us again to a living hope through the resurrection of Jesus Christ from the dead"*
> —1 Peter 1:3 NKJV

What we have in abundance (meaning "**boundless**") is God's GRACE and MERCY. The two go hand-in-hand, and there is no doubt that you have seen them used together more than once. Everything that God has given us can be summed up in these two words. But do we understand their significance or the difference between them?

The Foundation Stones
Repentance from Dead Works

GRACE is getting what you DON'T DESERVE.

MERCY is NOT getting what you DO DESERVE.

So by God's **mercy**, we escape the punishment that we deserve so abundantly (*"For the wages of sin is death"* Romans 6:23). But God does not stop there. By His **grace,** He also bestows on us in abundance the treasures of His love and provision. The whole of Jesus' redemptive work is summed up in this, for as sinners, we deserve the worst of all things and, instead, have been given EVERYTHING that is worth having.

Remember the warning in John 10:10 about the "thief" coming only to **steal** and **kill** and **destroy**? Look now at the second part of John 10:10 (NKJV): *"I have come that they may have life, and that they may have it more abundantly."* God's purpose in sending Jesus was that you and I might have **abundant life**. The only question is, are **we** going to BELIEVE it? The two parts of this verse actually work together, for when we begin to see how abundantly He has provided for us, we will not allow ourselves to be stolen from any longer. We will be able to recognize sin as a thief, stealing the presence and abundance of God from our lives.

- Ephesians 3:19 tells us that we are *"filled to the measure of all the fullness of God."*
- Romans 8:32 promises that God will *"graciously give us all things."*
- And Titus 3:6-7 says that through Jesus, *"we might become heirs having the hope of eternal life."*

WHETHER WE BELIEVE IT OR NOT!

The reality of these things may seem unreachable. But if we focus on the truth, we will eventually start to see THROUGH the truth! Draw these promises close and meditate on them until you can SEE them. Hold them constantly before your face. Then remind God of them until they become a reality in your life.

OUR FREEDOM IN CHRIST

Let's refer back to Genesis Chapter Three in order to identify the second deception. The serpent succeeded in causing Eve to lose sight not only of her **abundance** in God, but also her **FREEDOM** in Him. Satan has been diligent throughout history to remind Christians of the rules around which religion is structured. Our acceptance by God hinges on our ability to measure up to the guidelines, or so we are taught. But where does God say that we must get better before we come to Him?

Which are you more familiar with, the Ten Commandments or the **promises** of God? True enough, the Ten Commandments are from God's hands, and there is nothing wrong with knowing them. It is easier, after all, for us to understand and teach a list of dos and don'ts than the principle of grace. But is this why Jesus was sent to the Earth, to put us under a set of rules?

Galatians 5:1 tells us that *"It is for freedom that Christ has set us free."* Wonderful news, isn't it? It is not for works or service that we were set free, but for FREEDOM ITSELF!

This should be the focus of the Church, learning to walk in our freedom as the children of God, for the Bible tells us that *"where the Spirit of the Lord is, there is freedom"* (2 Corinthians 3:17). Instead, the concept of freedom stirs up a lot of controversy in religious circles, and so it is often **avoided** altogether. The Law can be viewed as a type of security blanket, strangely enough. Although it is harsh and unyielding, at least the boundaries are defined clearly, and the standard is set for all to see. Freedom in Christ, on the other hand, is awkward to us. It is often seen as nothing more than a "license to sin." After all, what is to keep you and me, when we KNOW that we have been set free, from taking advantage of it in pursuit of sinful desires? Take a look at the following verses:

"And I will put my Spirit in you and move you to follow my decrees and be careful to keep my laws." —Ezekiel 36:27

"I will put my laws in their minds and write them on their hearts."
—Hebrews 8:10 (see also 10:16)

You see, we do not need to be taught or to teach others a set of rules. For we already know that our best efforts apart from God are worthless to Him anyway. When we belong to God, He WRITES His laws on our hearts and minds. We are constrained and compelled and motivated by His love (and the leading of the Holy Spirit) and not by a set of guidelines. This is where true freedom comes from.

The first step toward freedom is to know and believe the truth, about God and about ourselves. Religion teaches only the No's, but the Bible tells us that "no matter how many promises God has made, they are 'Yes' in Christ" (2 Corinthians 1:20). If you desire freedom in your life, then take Jesus at His word, and see if He isn't faithful to it. For He challenged His followers, saying:

"If you hold to my teaching, you are really my disciples. Then you will know the truth, and the truth will set you free." —John 8:31-32

THE GOODNESS OF GOD

The third deception that the serpent set before Eve (and still sets before us today) deals with the character of God. The serpent convinced Eve that God had **held back** from her something that she needed. He cast a shadow on the heart of God, and Eve was quick to believe it.

The Foundation Stones
Repentance from Dead Works

Once again, we can identify with her response, for we have all experienced this to some degree. Have you ever doubted someone's heart toward you, even your closest friend, and found yourself pulling away out of self-preservation. In the same way, most of us spend our lifetimes RUNNING from God because we have no comprehension of His goodness. We believe the goodness of God is not **great enough** to:

> **accept us as we are**, so we strive to **do better**;
> **forgive us of our sins**, so we carry a load of guilt and shame;
> **love us unconditionally**, so we endeavor to earn it;
> **provide all that we need**, so we struggle to provide for ourselves.

The big question is this: Are we going to believe that **God is good,** or not? We will never know the tenderness of His touch until we do, for we would not dare get close enough. Claim it until it becomes yours: "IT IS WRITTEN ..."

"Taste and see that the Lord is good; blessed is the one who takes refuge in him." —Psalm 34:8

NOTES:

The Foundation Stones
Repentance from Dead Works

GOD'S DIRECTION VS. MY DIRECTION

As we endeavor to wrap up our discussion on the first of our foundation stones, let's take a step back in order to see the bigger picture. **Repentance from Dead Works**, we have learned, is a tedious and ongoing process. Therefore, it is easy to get caught up in the day-to-day struggles with our sin nature and lose sight of God's purposes. Learning to turn to God is not an end in itself. Rather, it is a grand beginning. By repenting, we learn to recognize, understand, and be led by the Holy Spirit within us.

We have been trained to live by external influences, gathering information in order to choose our direction and make rational decisions. This intellectual approach to life has served us well in the spheres of science and math. The problem, however, is that it can hinder God's leading. As a matter of fact, **reasoning** is the strength of the human soul, and so it poses a substantial threat to our faith. God's ways are so much higher than ours that they will never fall in line with our rationale. That is why we can do all the "right things" as far as the world is concerned and still be completely outside of God's will.

> Psalm 103:7 tells us that God *"made known his ways to Moses, his deeds to the people of Israel."*
>
> And in Psalm 95:10, God says of the Israelites, *"They are a people whose hearts go astray, and they have not known my ways."*

What was the difference between Moses and the nation of Israel? Together they witnessed the miracles of God's deliverance and experienced His saving grace. But Israel saw only God's **hand** (His acts) while Moses learned God's **heart** (His ways). And while Moses was merited as a great man of faith, the pages of the Old Testament resound with the unfaithfulness of Israel. The nation of Israel strayed from God time and time again simply because they did not KNOW Him.

The Foundation Stones
Repentance from Dead Works

God's love for the Israelites may seem obvious to us. After all, their deliverance from Egypt was a grand show of God's affection. But let's imagine ourselves in a similar situation. Let's say that someone you **do not know** began to send you gifts. While you may appreciate and even desire such kindnesses, your loyalty toward that person probably would not run very deep. Most likely, it would be contingent on the flow of the blessings themselves. For all you know of the person is what he or she has done for you and nothing of their love or devotion, much less their character. The nation of Israel was in this very spot (as are many of us today) because they experienced the blessings of God but did not know His heart for them. And if we seek God's blessings without seeking HIM, we will never come to know His heart for us either.

> *"My people are fools; they do not know me."* —Jeremiah 4:22

Let's take a look at Psalm 131, which was written by King David. David, *a man after God's own heart,* lays out for us in this psalm a wonderful example of what it means to truly know God's heart.

> *"My heart is not proud, Lord, my eyes are not haughty; I do not concern myself with great matters or things too wonderful for me. But I have calmed and quieted myself, I am like a weaned child with its mother; like a weaned child I am content."* —Psalm 131:1-2

Imagine the most renowned king in history confessing such a lowly position. He was neither proud of himself nor critical of others (haughty). He had surrendered his troubles to the hands of God, and he compared his soul to that of a weaned child with its mother. He had come to a place of total abandonment to his Father, and it held for him rest, contentment, and hope.

One might wonder how David (or anyone, for that matter) could learn to trust God so completely. We can be sure that an easy road is not the answer, for David's life was brimming with trials of grand proportions. David had pursued God's heart with a passion since he was a young shepherd boy, and

The Foundation Stones
Repentance from Dead Works

he knew beyond a shadow of a doubt that His God was a faithful, loving, and intensely personal God. As a child learns to trust the diligent and loving hands of a parent, so David had learned to trust the all-powerful hands of His Father.

Have you ever heard the term **"soulish" Christian**? It has been used to describe those who depend on themselves and other people (or things) for direction. Although they have been born again, they continue to live as the world does, being led by their souls (mind, emotions, and will). These people constantly find themselves reacting to circumstances, being driven by emotions, and struggling with anxiety over unresolved issues.

A **"Spirit-Led" Christian**, on the other hand, is directed not by feelings or reasoning at all but by God's truth and the Holy Spirit's directing. God moves the most in simplicity. We are called to simply be led by the Spirit of God and not to complicate life with anything but hearing Him. Our souls must be at rest (as we see in Psalm 131:1-2) in order to hear God.

Through repentance, we are essentially giving God control of our souls and choosing His ways over our own. When we learn to stop responding to our surroundings and, instead, obey the prompting of the Holy Spirit, God's Spirit becomes our inner direction. And a heart that is spontaneously being led by the Spirit is a heart that is sensitive to God and understands His ways. In short, this is God's purpose for you and me: to know Him deeply, to be led by Him easily, and to trust Him completely.

Ask yourself these three questions:

Do I refer to Him before I go or speak?

Am I quick to move independently of God?

Has my dependence on my ability to DO for God been broken?

Dependence on God is a hard lesson to learn. We must first be convinced of our need for it. Then it is a minute-by-minute struggle of the will, for we are always moving in one direction or the other. The good news, however, is that **perfection** is not the measuring line. We can never expect to be cured of our sinful natures. We are simply called to STAND on God's Word. Luke 21:19 tells us: *"Stand firm, and you will win life."* Our only responsibility is to TURN continually, and by **persevering** we will gain life. Furthermore, we learn God's ways through PATIENCE and CONSISTENCY in our faith, and the result is **stability** in our lives. Why? Because God does not change, and the truth of His Word provides a firm footing for us even in the midst of storms.

THE VOICE OF GOD

Ours has often been called the "fast-food generation" because we are accustomed to immediate gratification. We receive news from around the world as it is happening. We can travel to another country more quickly than people used to be able to travel to the next town. We can go through a drive-through for almost anything, and we are aggravated by the slightest delay. It is no wonder that we struggle to hear from God, for we simply do not have the patience.

In Scripture, we find very lengthy spans of time (sometimes hundreds of years) between God's conversations with His saints. God's desire is to make His will known, openly manifest, to you and me, but He does not operate according to our timetable. Therefore, we must learn to be steadfast and patient when seeking God.

Still, the business of hearing and being led by God can seem a little tricky and daunting at times. Most of us would be very hesitant to claim that we have heard from God about anything, and we would just as soon leave the whole matter to the spiritual giants of our time to sort out. But being led by the Spirit of God is neither mystical nor hit-and-miss, as we may assume. It is a privilege that has been given to each of His children, and it should be our defining mark as Christians. Romans 8:14 tells us that *"those who are*

The Foundation Stones
Repentance from Dead Works

led by the Spirit of God are children of God." The problem for most of us is that we are not familiar with His voice.

> *"Very truly I tell you Pharisees, anyone who does not enter the sheep pen by the gate, but climbs in by some other way, is a thief and a robber. The one who enters by the gate is the shepherd of the sheep. The gatekeeper opens the gate for him, and the sheep listen to his voice. He calls his own sheep by name and leads them out. When he has brought out all his own, he goes on ahead of them, and his sheep follow him because they know his voice. But they will never follow a stranger; in fact, they will run away from him because they do not recognize a stranger's voice."* —John 10:1-5

In the verse above, the "gate" that is referred to is the door to our hearts. We are the "watchmen," and our job is to guard our hearts from the lies of the enemy. But, as you see, we must first be able to tell the difference between the voice of God and the voice of a stranger. Repentence, essentially, is the means by which we become familiar with the Shepherd's voice. God's will is that we KNOW His voice so well that we can recognize the voice of "a stranger" (the enemy) immediately. Through consistency in our walk with Christ, we can immediately detect thoughts that come in the wrong way.

A bank teller must be very familiar with the look and feel of a genuine dollar bill. Not only would it be impossible do so with every type of counterfeit money, it would be unnecessary. For as long as she can be sure of the genuine article, she will not be fooled by anything less. It is the same way with hearing God's voice. If we really know Him, we will also know a counterfeit.

We all have the ability to hear from God because of the Holy Spirit within us (we are *"those who have ears,"* as Jesus said). But like a radio station that is not quite tuned in, most of us do not hear God's voice clearly. We listen to the lies of "thieves and robbers" many times and do not even realize it. God's desire is to give us clear direction. It is just a question of whether or not we are willing to receive it.

"I will lead the blind by ways they have not known, along unfamiliar paths I will guide them; I will turn the darkness into light before them and make the rough places smooth. These are the things I will do; I will not forsake them." —Isaiah 42:16

The Holy Spirit was given to us as a Guide and Helper. His job, according to John 16:13, is to *"guide you into all truth."* Sometimes we are led down paths that we do not understand. That is why it is very important that we are sensitive to His leading.

In Acts 16:6-8, we read that the Spirit of God kept Paul from preaching to or even entering certain provinces on his missionary journeys. God did not provide the reason for this, to Paul or to the readers of Acts, but we can be sure He had a purpose. Also, in Acts 10:19-20, we find an instance in which God directed Peter to the house of a Gentile (which was unheard of in Peter's day) immediately following a vision by which God corrected an age-old mentality regarding "unclean" foods. God's leading seemed to go against the teachings of the Bible (at least the Old Testament), but God was doing something new, even to Peter. When we begin to respond to and become familiar with God's leading inside of us, then we can say with confidence, "God has spoken," despite our circumstances.

The book of Proverbs, as you may already know, is believed to be a letter of wisdom and guidance that was written by a father (most likely King Solomon) to his son. It is a down-to-earth book that provides us with great insight into the practical outworkings of our faith. We are going to spend some time studying Proverbs 3:1-12, which deals specifically with the leading of God in our lives.

The Foundation Stones
Repentance from Dead Works

> ### Proverbs 3:1-4
> *"My son, do not forget my teaching, but keep my commands in your heart, for they will prolong your life many years and bring you peace and prosperity. Let love and faithfulness never leave you; bind them around your neck, write them on the tablet of your heart. Then you will win favor and a good name in the sight of God and man."*

The first four verses make it clear that **God directs us through His Word.** The Bible (God's Word) is the means by which we learn of His character, His love for us, His promises, and our very identity. There is no lasting trust in God's directing hand without the Word. And we are easily deceived by our very ignorance of the truth.

It is by God's Word that we are directed:

"Your word is a lamp for my feet, a light on my path."
—Psalm 119:105

The truth of God's Word—when we KNOW it and LIVE it— will keep us from deception:

"[M]y people are destroyed from lack of knowledge." —Hosea 4:6

Without the Word there is no faith:

" So then faith comes by hearing and hearing by the word of God. "
—Romans 10:17 (NKJV), Also James 1:22

> ## Proverbs 3:5-6
>
> *"Trust in the Lord with all your heart and lean not on your own understanding; in all your ways submit to him, and He will make your paths straight."*

Proverbs 3:5 tells us that **God will direct us when we trust Him to**.

- **Trust** – to confide, to be secure from fear. Firm belief in the honesty, truthfulness, justice and power of a person or thing.[4]

Ironically, our trust in God is developed through brokenness. It is only in our weakness as sinners that we can see His strength. Many people assume that Christians are supposed to be *better than* other people (which explains their disappointment when we fail). The truth is that we fall down just the same, except we have the power of God's grace to pick us back up. As Christians, our failures amount to nothing more than opportunities to trust in Him.

Have you ever been dared to fall backwards into someone's waiting arms? It is amazing how difficult it can be to trust even a dear friend with your well-being in such a situation. After all, you must be certain not only that the person would not intentionally let go but that he or she has the ability and strength to catch you. Trusting God with our lives is not much different. We must certainly be sure of His HEART for us and likewise be confident in His ABILITY and POWER.

- First, evaluate God's heart for you. Is He going to let you fall?
- Second, do you believe that God has the ability to take care of consequences, to keep you and save you?
- And last, is He strong enough to catch you?

The Foundation Stones
Repentance from Dead Works

When we truly trust God to direct, we will not fear:

"There is no fear in love. But perfect love drives out fear."
—1 John 4:18

"God is our refuge and strength, an ever-present help in trouble. Therefore we will not fear." —Psalm 46:1-2

We are called not just to trust, but to trust wholeheartedly:

"You will seek me and find me when you seek me with all your heart."
—Jeremiah 29:13

"Blessed are those who keep his statutes and seek him with all their heart." —Psalm 119:2

Matthew 6:25-34 talks about WORRY, which is essentially the opposite of trust. In this rather well-known exhortation, Jesus tells us that it is foolish to worry about our **daily needs**, for our Heavenly Father provides for even the birds of the air and the flowers of the fields. He warns us not to get caught up in the **concerns for the future**, for *"tomorrow will worry about itself"* (v. 34). God's Word also tells us that we must leave **our pasts** in God's hands and not allow them to dictate our futures. In Philippians 3:13, Paul makes the statement, *"But one thing I do: Forgetting what is behind and straining toward what is ahead ..."*

Why do we feel such a **need** to worry even when we know that it does more harm than good? It is because we are not comfortable living in the here-and-now. The strength of the soulish mind is planning, and past regrets are the preoccupation of our hearts. But we are not to LEAN (support ourselves) on our own understanding or abilities but to trust in God. The Holy Spirit leads us CURRENTLY, and until we have entrusted our yesterdays, todays, and tomorrows to God, we will miss Him every time. Keep in mind that the Holy Spirit is more concerned with teaching us to trust Him than with giving us victories.

The word "ways" as it is used in Proverbs 3:6, refers to "a course of life or action." And to "acknowledge" God is "to refer to Him." **God has promised to DIRECT** (to make right, pleasant, and prosperous) **our paths as we refer to Him.**

Proverbs 14:12, as you may recall, tells us that *"There is a way that seems right to a man, but its end is the way of death"* (NKJV). We are in great NEED of God's direction.

Proverbs 3:7-12

"Do not be wise in your own eyes; fear the Lord and shun evil. This will bring health to your body and nourishment to your bones. Honor the Lord with your wealth, with the firstfruits of all your crops; then your barns will be filled to overflowing, and your vats will brim over with new wine. My son, do not despise the Lord's discipline, and do not resent his rebuke, because the Lord disciplines those he loves, as a father the son he delights in."

In Proverbs 3:7-12, we find several warnings and admonitions that pertain to acknowledging God's leading. First, we must be careful not to imagine that our own wisdom is keeping us. This warning comes from the pen of Solomon, who was himself the wisest of all men (as granted by God). Instead, **we are to acknowledge that it is God's hand that directs our steps.**

"Those who trust in themselves are fools, but those who walk in wisdom are kept safe." —Proverbs 28:26

The Foundation Stones
Repentance from Dead Works

> *"So, if you think you are standing firm, be careful that you don't fall!"*
> —1 Corinthians 10:12

> *"This is what the Lord says: 'Let not the wise boast of their wisdom or the strong boast of their strength or the rich boast of their riches, but let the one who boasts boast about this: that they have the understanding to know me, that I am the Lord, who exercises kindness, justice and righteousness on earth, for in these I delight,' declares the Lord."*
> —Jeremiah 9:23-24

> *"Lord, I know that people's lives are not their own; it is not for them to direct their steps."* —Jeremiah 10:23

Proverbs 3:11-12 deals with the issue of discipline. No matter how we try to get around this issue, the fact is that **God directs us through discipline at times**. Solomon encourages us not to despise the Lord's discipline but to welcome it. For God only disciplines those who belong to Him, and it is done with Fatherly love for the purpose of RIGHTEOUSNESS and DIRECTION:

> *"No discipline seems pleasant at the time, but painful. Later on, however, it produces a harvest of righteousness and peace for those who have been trained by it."* —Hebrews 12:11

> *"He cuts off every branch in me that bears no fruit, while every branch that does bear fruit he prunes so that it will be even more fruitful."* —John 15:2

This chapter contains many promises of blessings, including health, nourishment, and fruitfulness, for those who are directed by God. But all of these pale in the light of the promise below. For the promise of God's presence and strength is all we really need.

> *"The Lord makes firm the steps of the one who delights in him"*
> —Psalm 37:23

The Foundation Stones
Repentance from Dead Works

NOTES:

The Foundation Stones
Repentance from Dead Works

NOTES:

FAITH TOWARD GOD

FAITH TOWARD GOD

INTRODUCTION

We have now come to the second of six foundation stones of Christianity (as listed in Hebrews 5:12 through 6:2), "**Faith Toward God**." Faith is a concept with which most of us are familiar, at least in part. The word can be found in just about any arena, from secular music to product slogans, not to mention the spiritual dimensions. But there is much to know about the subject and especially as it pertains to our relationship with God. After all, faith is the basis of our Salvation as well as our Sanctification. So let's make sure that we have a basic understanding of what faith is and how it works before we continue.

> *"Now faith is the substance of things hoped for, the evidence of things not seen."* —Hebrews 11:1 (NKJV)

We serve a God whose face we have never seen and whose voice we have never heard audibly. We hope in a Salvation that we cannot prove and look forward to a heavenly Kingdom that we have never witnessed. Consequently, FAITH—believing in a reality that we cannot see with our eyes—is the backbone of the Christian walk. It is our faith that sets us apart from the world, and it is our faith that enables us to have a relationship with the living God. We are called to walk by faith alone, trusting in the truth of God's Word above all that is within and around us.

> *"And without faith it is impossible to please God, because anyone who comes to him must believe that he exists and that he rewards those who earnestly seek him."* —Hebrews 11:6

Faith is God-given.

If you have been following along through this teaching thus far, then you probably are not terribly surprised by the statement that faith is God-given. After all, we have found that almost everything we have talked about

The Foundation Stones
Faith Toward God

(including repentance itself) must be **received** from God. Just as we cannot earn grace or mercy (which makes them just that), we also cannot earn faith. The Bible tells us plainly that faith, too, is a *"gift of God"* (see Ephesians 2:8). And so we find ourselves once again in the place where God requires of us something that only He can give, another testimony to our dependence on Him. For, as the verse below confirms, He is not only the SOURCE of our faith, He is also the REFINER of it.

> *"[L]ooking unto Jesus, the author and finisher of our faith"*
> —Hebrews 12:2 (NKJV)

And the Bible also tells us that God has given each of us a **"measure of faith"** (Romans 12:3). None of us is without faith (as given by God). Rather, the problem is that we do not always act *"in accordance with"* the faith we have been given (as the verse suggests).

Faith must be toward God.

Whether or not you realize it, you act on the principal of faith each and every day. You have faith in: your **car** (that it will get you to work), your **chair** (that it will hold you up), your **employer** (that he will pay you for your labor), etc. Do you get the idea? We cannot operate in this world without some level of faith. The real question is, ***in what do you invest your faith?***

> We exhibit *faith* every day. But what we put our faith in has eternal bearings.

Ultimately, it is **what we put our faith in** that matters. It does not take very long to learn that people and things are not worthy of total trust, for this is a fallen world full of imperfect people. Even the noblest of intentions cannot compensate for our sinful nature, and we will find ourselves disappointed time and time again.

The Foundation Stones
Faith Toward God

> *"This is what the Lord says: 'Cursed is the one who trusts in man, who draws strength from mere flesh and whose heart turns away from the Lord. ... But blessed is the one who trusts in the Lord, whose confidence is in him.'"* —Jeremiah 17:5-7

The harder lesson to learn is that we cannot trust in ourselves either. It is so easy to put our faith in our **abilities** because we can control the outcome (or so we think). We imagine ourselves ABLE to feel, reason, or perform our way through life, all the while missing God. We may even go so far as to put our faith in what we perceive as **OUR ABILITY** TO BELIEVE in God but never experience faith in God Himself. And we wonder why failure is so frustrating to us. We must learn that to fail is to simply fulfill God's expectation of us (apart from Him).

Have you ever been thrown into a tailspin by unexpected circumstances? It is amazing how much security we find in our plans. We can shrug off our hopes all we want to, but the disappointment that we experience when circumstances turn sour is a telltale sign that our faith had been misplaced. Take a look at the following verse. It describes the faith that is toward God, in spite of circumstances.

> *"Though the fig tree does not bud and there are no grapes on the vines, though the olive crop fails and the fields produce no food, though there are no sheep in the pen and no cattle in the stalls, yet I will rejoice in the Lord, I will be joyful in God my Savior. The Sovereign Lord is my strength; he makes my feet like the feet of a deer, he enables me to tread on the heights."* —Habakkuk 3:17-19

You see, faith not only comes FROM God, but it must also be TOWARD Him. The moment we start to take it upon ourselves, we will fall.

In Mark 11:22-24, Jesus talks to his disciples regarding the power of faith, using the example of a mountain being thrown into the sea in response to faith. But immediately beforehand, he simply says, *"Have faith in God,"* almost as a reminder that our faith must always be toward God. It is His hand that actually moves the mountains in response to our faith.

How do we know if we are really putting our faith in God? It is through times of trial that God allows us to see just that. The only secure foundation is in Him, and we can be sure that any instability that surfaces in our lives is the result of misdirected faith. Look, for example, at the verse below.

> *"Have mercy on me, my God, have mercy on me, for in you I take refuge. I will take refuge in the shadow of your wings until the disaster has passed. I cry out to God Most High, to God, who vindicates me. He sends from heaven and saves me, rebuking those who hotly pursue me—God sends forth his love and his faithfulness."*
> —Psalm 57:1-3

David wrote this psalm even as he fled for his life from King Saul. The entire psalm is filled with anguished cries and, at the same time, unspeakable faith in God. Faith is not a problem-solver but, rather, the means by which we soar above the tumult of life. Faith is clinging to God IN SPITE OF all else. And it is best learned when **all else** is pressing in on us.

The only way we can see the direction of the weathervane is by the force of the wind. The stronger the wind blows against it, the more steadily does it point in the true direction. So it is with our faith. The stronger the opposition, the more we point to Him.

Faith depends on the Word.

Faith must be based on the Word of God simply because it is the means by which we come to know our Father. After all, how could we have faith in God's saving grace, His love, His promises, etc. if we knew nothing about them? Romans 10:17 (NKJV) tells us that *"faith comes by hearing, and hearing by the word of God."* Furthermore, the book of John tells us that God's Word was *"written that you may believe"* (John 20:31).

The Foundation Stones
   Faith Toward God

There is still a link missing in this connection, however, for there are many skeptics who have studied the Bible from cover to cover without an ounce of faith resulting. It is not so much the KNOWING of God's Word that produces faith but our OBEDIENCE to it.

> **Obedience to the Word is the catalyst of faith.**

*"Why do you call me, 'Lord, Lord,' and do not do what I say? As for everyone who **comes to me** and **hears my words** and **puts them into practice**, I will show you what they are like. They are like a man building a house, who dug down deep and laid the foundation on rock. When a flood came, the torrent struck that house but could not shake it, because it was well built. But the one who hears my words and does not put them into practice is like a man who built a house on the ground without a foundation. The moment the torrent struck that house, it collapsed and its destruction was complete."*
                              —Luke 6:46-49 (emphasis added)

As this Scripture reveals, hearing (and even knowing) the Word of God is not enough. Only those who ACT ON the truth experience the security of faith in God. And this is where we most often find ourselves, at the crossroads of experience and faith. We cannot rely on our experience to prove the Word of God to us. **Rather, our experience is CREATED BY the Word of God when we step out in faith.**

We must learn to **claim** the promises of God by faith. It is then that we will see the evidence of faith's workings in our lives. Luke 1:38 (KJV) records Mary's words of faith that we can all claim for ourselves: *"[B]e it unto me according to thy word."*

God said it. I believed it. And that settles it!

If we are not relying on God's Word, then we are essentially operating on the principal of **PRESUMPTION** and not faith.

- **Presume** – To take for granted, assume to be true until disproved; to take upon oneself without warrant or permission; to suppose to be true without proof.[4]

We cannot presume victories from God. We must come to Him fresh every day with faith and a willingness to be instructed in the truth. For even God's angels harken to His Word:

> *"Bless the Lord, you His angels, who excel in strength, who do his word, heeding the voice of His word."* —Psalm 103:20 (NKJV)

Faith is increased when it is exercised.

We mentioned earlier that trials are a good way to find out what (or who) we have put our faith in. But there is more to our trials than just the exposure that they bring. When Satan tempts us in the area of our faith, he is not testing God's Word (for he knows better). Rather, he is trying to tempt us to let go of the faith that we do possess. But, if we stand firm in the truth, God can use times of testing to strengthen our faith, making faith **part of us** instead of something we are grasping for.

We are all given a certain measure of faith, but our faith should never grow stagnant. As I put the faith I already have (no matter how insignificant) in God, He will increase my faith in other areas. While it is sin to come to God with doubt in our hearts (unbelief), there is no condemnation in offering up our little faith. It is God's desire to increase it. Take a look, for example, at the account of the boy with the evil spirit (Mark 9:14-24). When Jesus spoke with the boy's father about having faith that he could heal, the father replied, *"I do believe; help me overcome my unbelief!"* We can—and need to—do the same each and every day. If you do not have faith in a particular area, come to God with the faith you do have, and trust Him for an increase.

The Foundation Stones
Faith Toward God

Faith is not for ourselves but others.

In reading Luke 17:5-10, we find that an interesting connection was made by Jesus concerning faith. In answer to His apostles' plea to *"increase our faith,"* Jesus proceeded with the well-known mustard-seed analogy. The apostles were most likely caught up in the imagery and overwhelmed by the revelation of faith's power. But notice that Jesus continues directly into a completely unrelated (or so it seems) topic. He endeavors to describe the mindset of the "unworthy servant" who counts himself so because he has done only his duty and no more.

What do you suppose Jesus meant to convey by linking the two together? Think about it for a moment. What is God's purpose in giving us faith? It is not so much for our own edification or understanding as it is for others. It is by faith that we serve others and glorify God. In short, as our faith increases, so does our willingness to serve those around us. Faith enables us to be a greater servant (in the order of THE "Servant of All," Jesus Christ). And God can accomplish more through a servant's heart than He can through the moving of any mountain.

NOTES:

FAITH'S SIGHT

> *"Now faith is confidence in what we hope for and assurance about what we do not see."* —Hebrews 11:1

If we were honest, most of us would have to admit that faith in God is not a particularly comfortable subject. We have a tendency to associate faith with walking blindly or in darkness, neither of which we are accustomed to. And maybe that is why we do not pursue the riches of faith the way we should. The reality of such a walk seems to be beyond our reach (and maybe beyond our desires as well).

Faith, in actuality, has nothing to do with blindness. Rather, it has everything to do with SIGHT, that is, **spiritual sight**. If you were to read the rest of Hebrews Chapter 11 (the famous "Faith Chapter") and through the first two verses of Chapter 12, you would be able to count thirteen references to SIGHT. This alone should give us a good indication that faith is not exactly what we imagine it to be.

> *"So we fix our eyes not on what is seen, but on what is unseen, since what is seen is temporary, but what is unseen is eternal."*
> —2 Corinthians 4:18

The verse above makes a clear distinction between what we would normally refer to as sight (physical) and a sight that is strictly SPIRITUAL. We naturally default to the first, but faith calls us to put aside what we see with our eyes in order to focus our **spiritual eyes** on the unseen (eternal).

Spiritual sight has to do with seeing through God's eyes. God opens our spiritual eyes (through revelation) to be able to see what we cannot naturally see. His ultimate goal is to change our perception of ourselves, the world around us, and Him.

The Foundation Stones
  Faith Toward God

And it is not really a matter of simply witnessing the fulfillment of God's Word. It is being able to **see** it even before it comes to pass. Abraham, for example, walked by faith in the promises God had given him, even though he never saw them materialize in his lifetime. He SAW them, nevertheless, because he was looking through the eyes of faith.

> *"All these people were still living by faith when they died. They did not receive the things promised; they only saw them and welcomed them from a distance."* —Hebrews 11:13

So we begin to see that faith is not walking blindly, neither is it groping in the darkness. Faith is about keeping our eyes on God, who is our Light in the darkness. Just as we must have light in order to see with our physical eyes, the same is true for spiritual sight. But, in this case, God is our source of light.

> **"God is light; in him there is no darkness at all.** *If we claim to have fellowship with him yet walk in the darkness, we lie and do not live by the truth. But if we walk in the light, as he is in the light, we have fellowship with one another, and the blood of Jesus, his Son, purifies us from all sin."* —1 John 1:5-7 (emphasis added)

According to the verse above, walking in darkness is proof that we do not live by the truth. In most cases, it is not that we do not have the light we need in order to walk by faith. **We just do not walk in the light that we have.** It is no different from knowing God's Word without DOING it. You may recall that when we do not hold onto a truth (by doing it), then we are destined to have it taken away from us. The same is true with spiritual light. If we do not walk in it, then we will lose it. And without light, we are actually **blinded** to the truth.

This very thing was true of the nation of Israel (as a whole). Romans 11:8 tells us that *"God gave them a spirit of stupor, eyes that could not see and ears that could not hear, to this very day."* This is the difference between those of

The Foundation Stones
Faith Toward God

us who are believers and those who are not. God has opened our eyes to the truth while unbelievers walk in darkness. They have not been given the ABILITY to see (spiritually) as we have. Look at the verses below:

> *"The god of this age has blinded the minds of unbelievers, so that they cannot see ... For God, who said, 'Let light shine out of darkness,' made his light shine in our hearts to give us the light of the knowledge of God's glory displayed in the face of Christ."*
> —2 Corinthians 4:4-6

> *"The path of the righteous is like the morning sun, shining ever brighter till the full light of day. But the way of the wicked is like deep darkness; they do not know what makes them stumble."*
> —Proverbs 4:18-19

How, you might be wondering, does God give us this light, which leads to spiritual sight? It is always through REVELATION of His Word. In Psalm 119:18 the psalmist pleads, *"Open my eyes that I may see wonderful things in your law."* Our need is actually two-fold. Obviously, we need God's Word, but we also need the Holy Spirit who reveals His Word to us. Anyone can read the Bible and gain an intellectual understanding of the truth. But it is only through revelation by the Spirit that the mysteries of God are brought to light in our hearts.

> *" 'What no eye has seen, what no ear has heard, and what no human mind has conceived'—the things God has prepared for those who love him—these are the things God has revealed to us by his Spirit"*
> —1 Corinthians 2:9-10

> *"The eye is the lamp of the body. If your eyes are healthy, your whole body will be full of light. But if your eyes are unhealthy, your whole body will be full of darkness. If then the light within you is darkness, how great is that darkness!"* —Matthew 6:22-23

The Foundation Stones
  Faith Toward God

The verse above refers to the eye as the "lamp of the body." It is through our spiritual eyes that the light of God's Word finds its way into our hearts. If our "eyes" are good then we will be full of the light of truth. But any lack in our spiritual sight results in profound darkness.

In the last lesson, we learned that faith is given to us not for our own benefit or edification, but for others. The spiritual light that accompanies faith is meant to illuminate our paths, for certain, but it is also to shine in the darkness as a beacon for others. God causes His light to shine from within us, and in so doing, He has made us the *"light of the world"* (see Matthew 5:14).

Philippians 2:15 says that in *"a warped and crooked generation"* we (those who walk in the truth) *"shine among them like stars in the sky."* Have you ever noticed that the darkness of night seems to magnify the brilliance of the stars? Similarly, the darkness of this world provides the perfect backdrop for God's light to shine through us. We are to radiate with light simply because we belong to the One who IS Light (see 1 John 1:5). Although we once belonged to the darkness, it no longer has a hold on us, and we should live as if we believe it!

> *"For you were once darkness, but now you are light in the Lord. Live as children of light."* —Ephesians 5:8

> *"You are all children of the light and children of the day. We do not belong to the night or to the darkness."* —1 Thessalonians 5:5

NOTES:

THE CREATIVE POWER OF GOD'S WORD

"By faith we understand that the universe was formed at God's command, so that what is seen was not made out of what was visible."
—Hebrews 11:3

"For he spoke, and it came to be; he commanded, and it stood firm."
—Psalm 33:9

We are all, no doubt, quite familiar with the creation account as told in Genesis. It is said that God **SPOKE** all of creation into existence, essentially forming it out of **nothing**. And we marvel at the thought of it. It is purely by FAITH (as the verse above says) that we believe that such a thing actually happened. After all, we cannot hope to understand an occurrence that defies the laws of science and math, not to mention the parameters of our experience.

The thing to remember when reading God's Word is that it was not given solely to inform about matters of historical significance. It was given to us that we may understand God's heart, His character, and His ways, which, by the way, NEVER CHANGE. Are we to assume, then, that God is still in the business of CREATING by His Word? Absolutely. God has **never** stopped speaking or creating.

- **Communication** – The act of imparting or transmitting; the transmission of ideas or information by speech or writing.[4]

Long ago the communication of God's Word created LIFE in the literal sense. And it is still imparting and transmitting life today, creating it in the spiritual realm.

"The words I have spoken to you—they are full of the Spirit and life."
—John 6:63

The Foundation Stones
Faith Toward God

Think for a moment about the significance of Jesus' incarnation. Colossians 1:15 tells us: *"The Son is the image of the invisible God."* Simply stated, He is tangible evidence of a God that is otherwise unseen. Someone once said:

"Jesus was God revealed to the senses. God *was* before He was revealed to the senses."

Jesus left no question as to His oneness with God the Father. When the disciple Philip asked Him to show them the Father, Jesus answered: *"Don't you know me, Philip, even after I have been among you such a long time? Anyone who has seen me has seen the Father"* (John 14:8-9).

"The Son is the radiance of God's glory and the exact representation of his being, sustaining all things by his powerful word."
—Hebrews 1:3

But there is even more to the whole scenario that we must understand before we go on. The book of John (written by the apostle) testifies to the deity of Jesus in a very interesting way. He begins by identifying Jesus as **"the Word"** who was with God from the beginning and through whom all things were created. Then John goes on to say that "the Word" (Jesus) took the form of a man and lived among us. Look at the verse below:

"In the beginning was the Word, and the Word was with God, and the Word was God. *He was with God in the beginning.* **Through him all things were made;** *without him nothing was made that has been made. In him was life, and that life was the light of all mankind. The light shines in the darkness, but the darkness has not overcome it. … He was in the world, and though the world was made through him, the world did not recognize him. He came to that which was his own, but his own did not receive him. Yet to all who did receive him, to those who believed in his name, he gave the right to become children of God. … The Word became flesh and made his dwelling among us."*
—John 1:1-14 (emphasis added)

What we see is a testimony to the creative power of the Word of God not only in the creation act but in the person of Jesus who is the Word incarnate. And guess what, Jesus is being formed in you and me as well if we are born again! God is creating still, WITHIN US!!

Think, for a moment, about the influence that **words** have had on your life. We are often oblivious to the power of the words we speak, that is, until we are on the receiving end. A simple word can create fear, despair, hope, pain, laughter, joy, etc., within us instantly. And, whether you realize it or not, it is the imparted word that has molded your personality and formed your perception of yourself and others. We are all products of the words that have been spoken into our lives.

> **WORD** – **Creates an image**
> **HEART** – **Imprints the image**
> **MOUTH** – **Reflects the image**

An imparted word CREATES an image in our minds, somehow altering our view of ourselves or someone else. If we accept the word, then our heart IMPRINTS the image. It is then given place in our thoughts and beliefs, becoming a reality to us. And when it is in our hearts, it will be REFLECTED in our own words. In Matthew 12:34 (NKJV), Jesus tells us that *"out of the abundance of the heart the mouth speaks."* Therefore, our words testify to the images imprinted on our hearts.

It is not a difficult principal to understand. Even in secular arenas, it has been determined that **thoughts** (words we speak to ourselves) possess great power to negatively or positively influence our lives. "The Power of Positive Thinking," a process of teaching yourself to think positively about life in order to obtain a more pleasant perspective of all things, is the world's answer to the problem. There is no doubt that there is a great deal of logic to it. One might consider it a noble endeavor to learn to think "happy thoughts," but the fact is that simply changing your perception of the world does not change the reality of it. An untruth, whether it is positive or negative, is still an untruth!

The Foundation Stones
Faith Toward God

The power of God's Word, on the other hand, is very real. And there are two things that make the difference:

1. God's Word is TRUTH
(not just a collection of happy thoughts)

2. God's Word is able to CREATE in us what is spoken
(instead of simply encouraging us to hope for it)

It is not enough just to avoid negative patterns of thinking. We must think and speak according to the truth of God's Word. Only His words have the power to create in us what is not already there. Just as God spoke the universe into existence out of NOTHING, so His word—when we believe it and speak it—creates in us the joy, love, hope, patience, understanding, compassion, etc., that we cannot muster up ourselves. A little hard to believe? Maybe so. But, have you ever tried it?

It seems that we have an easier time believing in the power of negative input—because we have experienced it first hand—than that of God's input. We have all been transformed to some extent by the criticisms, harsh words, and pessimistic remarks of those around us. We live each day according to words that were spoken into our lives years ago, believing ourselves to be what others have observed. It is no wonder that God's outlook seems so foreign to us.

Take another look at the verse below:

> "**By faith** *we understand that the universe was formed at God's command, so that* **what is seen was not made out of what was visible.**"
> —Hebrews 11:3 (emphasis added)

We have already talked about faith in the context of **spiritual sight** (see 2 Corinthians 4:18). Hebrews 11:3 gives us a deeper understanding of the workings of faith. Essentially, this verse tells us that **faith brings what is not seen into reality to be seen BY GOD'S WORD**. They all tie together.

When faith and the Word of God are combined in practice, we see His truth becoming a reality in our lives.

The purpose of speaking God's Word is not just to **remind** ourselves of His love, His promises, our identity in Him, etc. It is done IN ORDER TO **CREATE** THESE THINGS IN US! God has given us ALL things in abundance—joy, peace, hope, etc. When we speak these truths over our lives (even when we do not **feel** them), they are created in us by the power of God's Word. Romans 4:17 tells us that God *"calls into being things that were not."* And you and I are no exception. God speaks His promises into existence!

In light of what has been said so far, let's consider the purpose of prayer. Oftentimes we assume that we pray in order to convince God to take away an affliction, smooth a difficult road, or deliver us from disagreeable circumstances. We plead with Him for relief and struggle to understand the purpose in it all. Most of the time, God's purposes have little to do with our actual situations. We are struggling on the level of circumstances while the real fight is for our minds and hearts. Look at the verse below:

> *"The weapons we fight with are not the weapons of the world. On the contrary, they have divine power to demolish strongholds. We demolish arguments and every pretension that sets itself up against the knowledge of God, and we take captive every thought to make it obedient to Christ."* —2 Corinthians 10:4-5

The battleground for each Christian is in the mind. We are at war with the "arguments" that stand in opposition to God's Word and vie for a place in our hearts. We are not called to struggle against the people and situations that seem to bring despair into our lives. Our struggle is against the despair itself, as well as the hopelessness, fear, unforgiveness, etc. (anything that is not of God). And, although we imagine ourselves powerless against them, the fact is that **WE are the ones who actually give these things place** by neglecting to guard our hearts and minds with the truth of God's Word.

The Foundation Stones
Faith Toward God

> *"My son, pay attention to what I say; turn your ear to my words. Do not let them out of your sight, keep them within your heart; for they are life to those who find them and health to one's whole body. Above all else, guard your heart, for everything you do flows from it."*
> —Proverbs 4:20-23

Our responsibility is simple. We are watchmen, called to guard the door to our hearts with God's Word. Guarding our hearts and minds may seem like a trivial matter but only because we do not understand the importance of it. If we were to be honest, most of us would have to admit that we have not been attentive to our thoughts and words (nor have we felt the need to). We have a tendency in our preoccupation with life to leave ourselves wide open for the lies of the enemy, and we allow ourselves to be persuaded by them continually.

How powerful can our thoughts really be? Proverbs 23:7 (KJV) tells us that as a man *"thinketh in his heart, so is he."* We will not merely BELIEVE the images that have been imprinted on our hearts by words, we will CONFORM to them. And so they actually affect everything about us, from our perception to our choices to our character.

Leaving our hearts unattended is comparable to taking our hands off of the steering wheel of a moving vehicle. It is not a matter of IF but rather **WHEN** you will crash. So we will be quickly led astray if we do not keep a diligent watch and a firm footing in the truth.

Sow a THOUGHT ☞	Reap a CHOICE
Sow a CHOICE ☞	Reap a HABIT
Sow a HABIT ☞	Reap a CHARACTER
Sow a CHARACTER ☞	Reap a DESTINY

Be determined to hold on to God's Word, even for a day. Cast down any negative thoughts that come in and speak the truth over them. You may be amazed by the struggle you will have in regaining your post, for the gate has probably been left unattended and wide open for some time. But in doing this you will witness the power of the truth in your life.

We must speak the truth over ourselves and ask God to create in us what He says is in us. And our part is to simply AGREE with Him!!

The Words of the Wise

"A person finds joy in giving an apt reply—and how good is a timely word!" —Proverbs 15:23

"A word aptly fitly is like apples of gold in settings of silver." —Proverbs 25:11 (NKJV)

"Words from the mouth of the wise are gracious, but fools are consumed by their own lips." —Ecclesiastes 10:12

"The hearts of the wise make their mouths prudent, and their lips promote instruction." —Proverbs 16:23

"The words of the wise are like goads, their collected sayings like firmly embedded nails – given by one Shepherd." —Ecclesiastes 12:11

"Let your conversation be always full of grace, seasoned with salt, so that you may know how to answer everyone." —Colossians 4:6

The Foundation Stones
Faith Toward God

THE PRINCIPLE OF CONFESSION

We have been talking about the creative power of God's Word, and now we will continue along the same lines with the principle of CONFESSION. The word "confession" seems to have taken on a negative connotation in today's world, probably because it is most often associated with asking forgiveness for specified sins. But the confession we are talking about today is confession of the truth of God's Word.

> *"It is written 'I believed; therefore I have spoken.' Since we have that same spirit of faith, we also believe and therefore speak."*
> —2 Corinthians 4:13

One important thing to remember about faith is that IT ALWAYS SPEAKS. What we put our faith in "speaks" every day simply because **we speak what we believe**. If we have put our faith in God, our mouths will reflect it. If our faith is in something (or someone) other than God, then that will be evident as well, through our words.

> *"For out of the abundance of the heart the mouth speaks."*
> —Matthew 12:34-37 (NKJV)

Any problems that become evident through my speech are actually rooted in my heart. For God reveals the condition of our hearts by our mouths. The mouth is nothing more than a red flag indicating the direction of the heart. It is a kind of gauge, as would be found in a car. The gauge is the **indicator** of a problem, and not the problem itself.

In light of the fact that our words are simply the product of our hearts, we can see that correcting our speech is not a remedy. As a matter of fact, it is not even a feasible option. For the Bible tells us that *"no human being can tame the tongue"* (see James 3:1-12). Our speech (or **confession**) is the result of our **beliefs**, which stem from our **thinking**, which is produced by

The Foundation Stones
Faith Toward God

our **knowledge**, which has its origin at our **SOURCE**. Once again, if the outcome is wrong, we must go back to the source. Let's take a look at the

SOURCE	KNOWLEDGE	THINKING	BELIEFS	CONFESSION
⇩	⇩	⇩	⇩	⇩
The Spirit	The Word	Meditation on The Word	According to the Word	Opinion of God

You may remember this sequence, only in a more general format, from a previous section. Hopefully, it will be helpful in understanding our current discussion on confession. You can see that our confession (or speech) is at the end of a progression that originates at the source (essentially the direction of our hearts). It would be backwards to alter our words or even our beliefs without going back to the root. As a matter of fact, any change that does not begin at the source is nothing more than CONFORMING. What God wants to do is TRANSFORM our hearts, and our tongues will follow accordingly. Let's take a closer look at this process in this diagram:

When our **SOURCE** is the **Spirit**,
then our **KNOWLEDGE** will be based on **The Word of God**.

• • •

When we **STUDY** The Word of God,
then our **THINKING** will be **Meditation on the Word**.

• • •

If we are **THINKING** on the Word,
then our **BELIEFS** will also be formed **According to the Word**.

• • •

And what comes out of our mouths
—our **CONFESSION**—
will naturally be **The Opinion of God**.

The Foundation Stones
Faith Toward God

As we said earlier, the principal of confession can be a confusing topic simply because we automatically assume that it has to do with admitting to a wrong. But that is not at all the type of confession we are talking about today. Take a look at the meaning of the word itself:

- **Confession** – Homologeo (#3670) [5]
    Homo = the same
    Logos = something spoken; to speak or say the same as the word

> **True confession is simply saying the same thing that God says about (others and) me.**

Confession, essentially, is the act of speaking and agreeing with the Word of God. It is the vehicle by which God's Word creates, as well as a very practical outworking of our faith.

> *"Do two walk together unless they have agreed to do so?"* —Amos 3:3

According to the verse above, we MUST agree with God if we are to ever "walk" with him. The alternative is that we are agreeing with the lies of the enemy and walking in deception. Our only responsibility, despite all else, is to line ourselves up with the Word of God, claiming "I am who God says I am!" I know it sounds too simple, but is that not why we often miss the things of God, because of their simplicity?

One thing we need to keep in mind when confessing God's Word is that God is not human. He cannot lie, nor does He change His mind (see Numbers 23:19 and Hebrews 6:18). If God said it, we can bank on it. The question is, are we willing to? Another important point to understand is that GOD HONORS OUR CONFESSIONS, whether they are truth or lies. **We will actually receive the things that we speak**, just as one reaps what he sows!

> *"So tell them, 'As surely as I live, declares the Lord, I will do to you the very thing I heard you say.'"* —Numbers 14:28

The Foundation Stones
Faith Toward God

The Bible tells us that we will eat the fruit of our mouths, that our very words bring about good things. Look at the verses below:

> *"From the fruit of their mouth a person's stomach is filled; with the harvest of their lips they are satisfied. The tongue has the power of life and death, and those who love it will eat its fruit."*
> —Proverbs 18:20-21

> **"From the fruit of their lips people enjoy good things."**
> —Proverbs 13:2

In the last section, we discussed the importance of guarding our hearts and minds, which is essentially checking the **source** of every thought that enters in. It is equally important that we guard our mouths. And remember that it is not simply a matter of training oneself to say the right things (conforming). We must seek to understand our hearts by our words and determine to speak (confess) the Word of God in all things. The Bible (and especially the book of Proverbs) has much to say about the subject:

> *"He who guards his lips guards his life, but he who speaks rashly will come to ruin."* —Proverbs 13:3

> *"Those who guard their mouths and their tongues keep themselves from calamity."* —Proverbs 21:23

Our prayer should be that of the psalmist who wrote, *"Set a guard over my mouth, Lord; keep watch over the door of my lips"* (Psalm 141:3). Only God is able to "instruct our tongues" so that we will speak LIFE to the hearts of others.

> *"The Sovereign Lord has given me an instructed tongue, to know the word that sustains the weary. He wakens me morning by morning, wakens my ears to listen like one being taught."* —Isaiah 50:4

The Foundation Stones
Faith Toward God

CONFESSING GOD'S WORD

We have spoken in previous chapters of the power of God's Word to create. His Words have created and still are creating, when we agree by faith in God's Word and speak them. The power of the Word is released to perform according to the Word.

Study these confessions below and keep those that apply to your life. Confess them, and be amazed how God can change both you and your circumstances.

Study God's Word and add other confessions to these.

CONFESSIONS BASED ON GOD'S WORD TO MEET MY NEEDS

- Thank You, Father, that You know what I am in need of before I even ask. Thank You that You have promised to supply all of my needs according to your riches in glory. Thank You that You have given us all things that pertain unto life and godliness.   (Philippians 4:19, 2 Peter 1:3)

- Father, I know You are able to bless me abundantly so that I can do Your will in my life.   (2 Corinthians 9:8)

- Thank You, Father, that I don't worry about my needs. You have supplied the needs of Your creation, and You will supply mine. I will seek Your kingdom, and all these things will be added to me.   (Matthew 6:25-34)

- Father, You gave us the very best by giving us Your Son, Jesus Christ. You would not hold back but freely give us all things.   (Romans 8:32)

- I am not anxious about anything. As I pray and confess Your Word, I am filled with thanksgiving and peace.   (Psalm 34:10)

CONFESSIONS FOR OVERCOMING FEAR AND WORRY

- Father, I realize that worry and fear are an attack on Your character, so instead of running away, I come to You, and You give me rest. I will learn of Your gentle and humble heart, and there I will find rest for my soul. (Matthew 11:28-30)

- You are the Prince of Peace. I will not let my heart be troubled. I trust in You today. (John 14:2)

- Thank You, Father, that I am surrounded by Your love, and nothing can separate me from it. (Romans 8:38-39)

- Thank You, Father, that even though I walk through some dark valleys, I have nothing to fear, for You are with me. Your rod and Your staff they comfort me. (Psalm 23:4)

CONFESSIONS FOR STRENGTH

- Father God you are my refuge and strength and an ever present help when I need you. (Psalm 46:1-3)

- There is nothing I cannot do as you give me strength. (Philippians 4:13)

- As I hope in you Lord, my strength is renewed and I will soar on wings like eagles; I will run and not grow weary. I will walk and not faint. (Isaiah 40:29-31)

- Your grace is sufficient for me. Even in my weakness I am learning to delight in these situations so that when I am weak you are strongest. (2 Corinthians 12:9-10)

- Thank you Lord that I am your child and greater is the one in me than the one in the world. (1 John 4:4)

The Foundation Stones
Faith Toward God

CONFESSIONS FOR WISDOM AND GUIDANCE

- Your Word says if I lack wisdom, I can ask and You will give it to me. I am asking now and believing, not doubting. Your wisdom is directing my steps. (James 1:5-7)

- Thank You, Heavenly Father, that You have given me the spirit of wisdom and revelation, my eyes have been enlightened, and I can know the hope you impart. I walk in the same power that raised my Lord Jesus from the dead. (Ephesians 1:17-21)

- Thank You, Father, for the wisdom given to me from Christ, for You are my wisdom, my righteousness, my holiness, and my redemption. (1 Corinthians 1:30)

- I walk in the wisdom from God, for it is pure and peace loving. (James 3:14-18)

- I know that the natural mind cannot receive the wisdom that God has for us, but we have the mind of Christ. The Holy Spirit reveals the understanding that I need. (1 Corinthians 2:11-16)

NOTES:

THE SPIRIT OF FAITH

You have been reading about the principle of confession and the power of the spoken Word of God in our lives. We have touched on the fact that our speech is a direct reflection of the condition of our hearts. It is important to understand that our tongues have the power of life and death (see Proverbs 18:20-21). And equally important is the realization that we cannot control our tongue. In the New Testament book that is named for him, James 3:8 concluded that *"no human being can tame the tongue."* And that is because what comes out of our mouths is simply the overflow of our hearts. Matthew 15:18 tells us, *"But the things that come out of a person's mouth come from the heart, and these defile them."* In other words, what comes out of the faucet is what is in the well.

But there is good news. God has already provided the answer to this vexing problem. We may feel utterly helpless to fix ourselves, but that is the point at which God is able to do it for us. God desires not just to correct our tongues or even our hearts. His plan is much grander. He has given you and me a new heart, and He has placed His Spirit within us to guide us along the path of truth.

> *"I will give you a new heart and put a new spirit in you; I will remove from you your heart of stone and give you a heart of flesh. And I will put my Spirit in you and move you to follow my decrees and be careful to keep my laws."* —Ezekiel 36:24-27

Our faith, you see, is not born out of conformity. Rather it is a product of the new heart and new spirit that God has given us, His children. To walk by faith is to be led by the Spirit of God as our hearts are constrained by His love.

We have identified that our hearts are motivated by our SOURCE, that being either the truth or a lie. But we could also say that our source is a

spiritual influence. For as surely as the Spirit of God brings the truth, so is our spiritual enemy (the "father of lies") behind all deception. While believers cannot be demon-possessed, they can certainly be demon-affected. And if you have ever found yourself being driven by fear, frustration, unbelief, or the like, then you have experienced this very thing.

The mind, emotion, and will (the soul) are all empowered by the same source, and God will allow times of testing in our lives in order to reveal what spirit is motivating us. And, once again, it is our mouths that betray us. For whatever we believe, we will speak.

> *"It is written: 'I believed; therefore I have spoken.' Since we have **that same spirit of faith**, we also believe and therefore speak"*
> —2 Corinthians 4:13 (emphasis added)

The great men of God spoken of in the Bible all had this in common: they knew their source. And it was with the **spirit of faith** that they BELIEVED and therefore spoke. In Psalm 116:10 (NKJV), King David wrote, *"I believed, therefore I spoke"* and by this principle he lived. He was motivated in all that he did by the spirit of faith that is spoken of in the verse above. Likewise, we are called to be motivated by the same spirit of faith, always being conscious of our source.

Our source affects our VISION, our WALK, and our TALK. We have already talked at great length about how our confession (our talk) is a reflection of our source. But there is more to the walk of faith than speaking according to the truth. It is by the spirit of faith that we are also able to see through God's eyes and overcome in our daily walk.

SEEING THROUGH GOD'S EYES

One of the more popular Biblical accounts of spiritual sight can be found in 2 Kings 6:8-23. We are told that the prophet Elisha, along with his servant boy, awoke one morning to the sight of an army with horses and chariots surrounding his city in pursuit of him, no less. His servant responded with panic. But Elisha replied, *"Don't be afraid. Those who are with us are more than those who are with them"* (v. 16). Now, we can safely assume that either Elisha was out on a limb of presumption, OR that he could **see** something that the boy did not. When we read the next verse, we find that the latter is true:

> *"And Elisha prayed, 'Open his eyes, Lord, so that he may see.' Then the Lord opened the servant's eyes, and he looked and saw the hills full of horses and chariots of fire all around Elisha."*
> —2 Kings 6:17

Elisha was certainly a man who walked by the spirit of faith, and God granted him spiritual sight that worked out in very practical, even thrilling, ways. While we may never experience a vision of chariots of fire, there is still a very real spiritual sight that comes through faith. It is the experience of seeing through God's eyes, of looking beyond the natural to those things that are unseen.

> *"So we fix our eyes not on what is seen, but on what is unseen, since what is seen is temporary, but what is unseen is eternal."*
> —2 Corinthians 4:18

Paul prayed for this very thing in his letter to the Ephesians. He asked that God would give them the eyes of understanding in order that they may know *"the **hope** to which he has called you, the **riches** of his glorious inheritance in his holy people, and his incomparably great **power** for us who believe"* (see Ephesians 1:17-21 [emphasis added]). For if we cannot SEE these things, we will never understand who we are in Christ, the promises that have been given us, or our authority as children of God. Without spiritual sight, we are already deceived.

Hebrews 11:1 tells us that *"faith is confidence in **what we hope for** and assurance about **what we do not see**"* (emphasis added). And there is something significant about that statement. For it can be said that our hope

The Foundation Stones
Faith Toward God

TODAY is what causes us to see God TOMORROW. Many of us **know** and **believe** the promises of God. We may even be in the habit of sharing them with others. But how consistently do we **step out in believing without first seeing**? Without this element of faith, we are forever caught in a loop of disillusionment. For a spirit of faith generates hope and enables us to see "what we do not see." The absence of it, however, leads to hopelessness and spiritual blindness.

When the Israelites were delivered from Egypt and brought to the border of Canaan (the Promised Land), there were spies sent into the land to assess the situation. All but two of the men, upon returning, reported the overwhelming strength and size of their adversaries. They claimed: *"We seemed like grasshoppers in our own eyes, and we looked the same to them"* (Numbers 13:33).

Now the important thing to remember is that God had promised the Israelites the land that lay before them. Yet, they saw themselves and their situation through their own eyes instead of God's. They believed a lie and acted according to a spirit of fear and intimidation.

And notice also that the Canaanites saw the Israelites **as they saw themselves** *("like grasshoppers")*. Isn't that interesting? It seems that when we see ourselves in a certain light, others tend to do the same. If we believe that we are backwards, incapable, or unattractive, we will likely portray that very image to others. Think about this in terms of the spiritual world. The lies of the enemy are the source of our identity until we choose to believe the truth. And, although Satan KNOWS who we really are in Christ, his objective is to keep us convinced of our inadequacy. He will never treat us better than we see ourselves, and that is why he is after our sight. For as long as we reject God's perspective, we will not walk in the authority that has been given us.

On the other hand, look at the response of Caleb, who saw with his eyes the very same "giants" that the others had. He told the people, *"We should go up and take possession of the land, for we can certainly do it"* (Numbers 13:30). What made the difference in Caleb's mind? FAITH. He was walking by the spirit of faith, believing that **God** was able to do what He said He would do. And God moved mightily on behalf of Caleb for this reason.

> *"But because my servant Caleb has a different spirit and follows me wholeheartedly, I will bring him into the land he went to, and his descendants will inherit it."* —Numbers 14:24

Caleb's "different spirit" enabled him to see through God's eyes. While others saw giants on their Promised Land, Caleb saw an opportunity for God to deliver them. It was his spiritual sight that motivated his hope. Such was also the case with Moses, who, according to Hebrews 11:27, *"persevered because he saw him who is invisible."* And it is this confidence that enables us to OVERCOME, as we will see next.

OVERCOMING IN OUR WALK

Most people would be hesitant to claim that they are **overcomers** simply because we do not often experience the reality of it. But we have to remember that the truth of God's Word goes beyond our feelings, our experience, and sometimes even beyond our comprehension. If God has said something, we should not be so quick to dismiss it, no matter how foreign it may seem. And the following verse may very well fall into this category for most of us.

> *"[F]or **everyone** born of God overcomes the world. This is the victory that has overcome the world, even our faith. Who is it that overcomes the world? Only the one who believes that Jesus is the Son of God."*
> —1 John 5:4-5 (emphasis added)

Did you catch the significance of that statement? Firstly, the verse tells us that EVERYONE who is born again is an overcomer. And it goes on to explain that **it is the faith within us that overcomes the world!** That is to

The Foundation Stones
   Faith Toward God

say that the Spirit of God within us produces the faith in us that **will** overcome. And, whether we realize it or not, our faith overcomes the world WITHIN us continually.

This is where the power of the spoken Word of God comes back into play. When we can **see** and **speak** in faith, then we will overcome by faith. When we walk according to the spirit of faith, we will be willing to fight for the promises of God (as Caleb was), and the words of our testimony will silence the accusations of the enemy.

> *"Then I heard a loud voice in heaven say: 'Now have come the salvation and the power and the kingdom of our God, and the authority of his Messiah. For the accuser of our brothers and sisters, who accuses them before our God day and night, has been hurled down. They triumphed over him by the blood of the Lamb and by* **the word of their testimony.**'"
> —Revelation 12:10-11 (emphasis added)

NOTES:

THE NEARNESS OF GOD'S WORD

We have a tendency as Christians to imagine the things of God to be just out of our reach. We strive for holiness, obedience, righteousness, etc., but never seem to attain them. And what's more, many of us conclude that this scenario is by God's design—a means by which He keeps us at arm's length and always hungry for more. And maybe that is why we are resigned to the "if only God would ..." mentality that we find ourselves drowning in.

The tragedy of this condition is twofold. For one, it does a great injustice to the heart of God. After all, it is nearly impossible to reconcile the loving and compassionate God of the Bible with the distant and uncaring image we have of Him. Secondly, it is a deception of the worst kind. If we are still WAITING for God to **come near** to us, then we have overlooked His coming. His Holy Spirit and the truth of His Word are WITHIN us and ever-present.

> *"But the righteousness that is by faith says: 'Do not say in your heart, "Who will ascend into heaven?"' (that is, to bring Christ down) 'or "Who will descend into the deep?"' (that is, to bring Christ up from the dead). But what does it say? '**The word is near you; it is in your mouth and in your heart**,' that is, the message concerning faith that we proclaim."* —Romans 10:6-8 (emphasis added)

> *"Now what I am commanding you today is not too difficult for you or beyond your reach. It is not up in heaven, so that you have to ask, 'Who will ascend into heaven to get it and proclaim it to us so we may obey it?' Nor is it beyond the sea, so that you have to ask, 'Who will cross the sea to get it and proclaim it to us so we may obey it?' **No, the word is very near you; it is in your mouth and in your heart so you may obey it**."* —Deuteronomy 30:11-14 (emphasis added)

The Foundation Stones
Faith Toward God

Let's take a look at the men and women of faith whom the Old Testament speaks about. Hebrews 11:13 tells us that *"All of these people were still living by faith when they died. They did not receive the things promised; they only saw them and welcomed them* **from a distance**" (emphasis added). While this is the case for those who lived before the coming of Christ, we certainly cannot say the same for ourselves. Look at the following verse (still speaking of the saints of old) which may help to explain why this is so:

> *"These were all commended for their faith, yet none of them received what had been promised, since* **God had planned something better for us** *so that only together with us would they be made perfect."*
> —Hebrews 11:39-40 (emphasis added)

Many of **us** are **looking forward** to the promises of God and missing the fact that THEY HAVE ALREADY BEEN FULFILLED! What these men and women were waiting for is ours today through the blood of Christ.

Before the coming of Christ, God's children were governed by the Old Covenant (the LAW). It brought recognition of sin but along with it **condemnation** and **death**. It was meant to point us to God without the power to reconcile us to Him. The Old Covenant was only a shadow of the covenant to come through Jesus Christ.

> *"For the law was given through Moses; grace and truth came through Jesus Christ."* —John 1:17

The New Covenant is the "something better" that God had planned for you and me. It is a covenant of **grace** and **truth** (as the verse above says). While the Old Covenant resulted in condemnation and death, the New Covenant brings forth righteousness and life (all that we are striving for) through simple faith.

> *"If the ministry that brought condemnation was glorious, how much more glorious is the ministry that brings righteousness!"* —2 Corinthians 3:9

So we find that through the New Covenant of Christ's blood, we CURRENTLY walk in the fulfillment of God's promises, those that the saints could only look forward to. We are no longer alienated and kept at a distance from God. Rather, we have been "brought near."

> *"But now in Christ Jesus you who once were far away have been brought near by the blood of Christ."* —Ephesians 2:13

As a matter of fact, Jesus' mission on this earth was to forever eliminate the distance (caused by sin) that lay between God and His children. 1 John 3:8 tells us that *"The reason the Son of God appeared was to destroy the devil's work."* And take a look also at the verse below:

> *"Since the children have flesh and blood, he too shared in their humanity so that by his death he might break the power of him who holds the power of death—that is, the devil"* —Hebrews 2:14

IS IT FINISHED?

Traditionally, an Old Testament priest was never to sit down while serving at the Temple. This was to symbolize that the atoning for sins was unending. The animals that were sacrificed were only a shadow of the ultimate sacrifice to be made by Jesus Christ. And, when this was done, the Bible tells us that Jesus (acting as our Priest) *"sat down at the right hand of God"* (see Hebrews 10:12-14) as a testimony to the finished work of Calvary. That is to say that His work was complete. The verse ends by stating, "by one sacrifice He has made perfect forever those who are being made holy."

The important thing to keep in mind is that the end of the book has already been written as far as our faith is concerned. Time may still be marching forward, but our fate is not hanging in the balance. When Jesus was breathing His last, He uttered the words, "It is finished!" Yes, His life on earth was finished, His mission was complete, and His pain was coming to

The Foundation Stones
Faith Toward God

an end. But His cry was really for our ears. It was a triumphant proclamation of God's victory in bridging the gap of sin and death. It was an assurance to you and me that nothing more needed to be done to make us righteous in the eyes of heaven. ALL provision has already been made for the children of God. There is nothing left for us to do but BELIEVE. And that is precisely what God requires of us.

Think of the Israelites as they teetered on the edge of the Promised Land. God had already set aside the land for them and assured them of total victory were they to claim it. We could say that it was fear and intimidation that caused them to walk away from their inheritance with no hope in their hearts. But it was really their UNBELIEF, for that is what gave place to the lies (see Hebrews Chapter 3). And such is the case with us. We may be convinced that we are spiritually inadequate to stand on the Word of God. But the truth is that we are simply not believing and resting in the provision that has already been made for us.

"Now we who have believed enter that rest."   —Hebrews 4:3

"Who has believed our message and to whom has the arm of the Lord been revealed? ... Surely he took up our pain and bore our suffering, yet we considered him punished by God, stricken by him, and afflicted."
—Isaiah 53:1, 4

And the interceding of Christ on our behalf continues even today. First John 2:1 tells us that *"we have an advocate with the Father—Jesus Christ, the Righteous One."* And so we can say with confidence that IT IS FINISHED. As the verse below tells us, we are saved **completely** by the blood of Christ.

"Therefore he is able to save completely those who come to God through him, because he always lives to intercede for them."
—Hebrews 7:25

The Foundation Stones
Faith Toward God

THE CIRCLE OF EXPERIENCE

At this point, we have learned the basic principals of faith well enough to be wondering one very important thing. If we ALL have a measure of faith, and if God desires to increase it, then why do we remain spiritual babies instead of growing to be mighty men and women of God? If faith is so powerful an instrument in our lives, then why do we not witness its influence more often than we do? Romans 10:17 tells us that *"faith comes from hearing the message, and the message is heard through the word about Christ."* So we know that:

THE WORD COMES
THEN
FAITH COMES

But what we often do not realize is that, at this point, **SATAN COMES** as well. He comes to steal the Word from our hearts before it has any lasting effect on our lives. Let's take a look at Jesus' explanation of a parable that you may be familiar with—the Parable of the Sower.

> *"This is the meaning of the parable: The seed is the word of God. **Those along the path** are the ones who hear, and then the devil comes and takes away the word from their hearts, so that they may not believe and be saved. **Those on rocky ground** are the ones who receive the word with joy when they hear it, but they have no root. They believe for a while, but in the time of testing they fall away. **The seed that fell among thorns** stands for those who hear, but as they go on their way they are choked by life's worries, riches and pleasures, and they do not mature. But **the seed on good soil** stands for those with a noble and good heart, who hear the word, retain it, and by persevering produce a crop."* —Luke 8:11-15 (emphasis added)

In this parable, you will notice that the problem is never the seed itself (God's Word), but rather the GROUND that it lands on (which is our hearts). There

The Foundation Stones
   Faith Toward God

are four different categories of people who are represented here:

The **first** allows the Word to be STOLEN by the enemy before it takes root.
The **second** embraces the Word but then LETS IT GO in the face of trials.
The **third** hears the Word but FINDS NO PLACE FOR IT among worldly concerns.
And, the **fourth** is the only "good soil" that ACCEPTS and RETAINS the Word through **perseverance**.

Where do you see yourself in this picture? The Word of God has been sown into each of our hearts by revelation. We have all held "seeds" of truth, which (if planted) have the ability to reproduce and multiply within us. What most of us do not understand is that these seeds do not become OURS until we claim them, guard them, and persevere in them. We expect God's Word to just **happen** to us, not realizing that our spiritual enemy is a whole lot more determined to take possession of our promises than we are.

James 1:21 instructs us to *"humbly accept the word planted in you, which can save you."* The important thing is not how much revelation you and I have received but how much REMAINS. And this is the key to maturing in faith by experience.

> *"If you hold to my teaching, you are really my disciples. Then you will know the truth, and the truth will set you free."* —John 8:31-32

Below are five basic steps that we must follow in order to experience the freedom that the verse above speaks about. It is the process of HOLDING TO the Word of God:

1. **Receive** (the revelation of God's Word – the seed)
2. **Choose** (to hold onto it)
3. **Determine** (the direction of obedience – game plan)
4. **Act** (in obedience to it)
5. **Continue** (sowing and reaping – a seasonal cycle)

The Foundation Stones
Faith Toward God

Genesis 1:12 reminds us of the basic truths of sowing and reaping. Simply speaking, seeds produce **according to kind**. If we sow a watermelon seed, we would never expect to find an apple tree growing from it. And this is true spiritually as well. If the truth is sown into our hearts, it will produce more of the same. The Word of God will always reproduce after God and create a correct image within us. And that is precisely why Satan is not willing to stand idle when the seeds of truth are in our possession. When Satan comes, it is never to test the Word of God; for he knows better than we do that the Word is true (see James 2:19). **He comes to test *our faith in it*!**

But the purposes of God shine through even in these scenarios. For Satan's goal is to shake the truth loose from our grip. But God can use this very thing to teach us to hold the truth more tightly. If the enemy is not victorious in his endeavors, then we are all the richer for the experience.

> *"And we glory in the hope of the glory of God. Not only so, but we also glory in our sufferings, because we know that suffering produces **perseverance**; perseverance, **character**; and character, **hope**. And hope does not put us to shame."* —Romans 5:2-5 (emphasis added)

We have a tendency as humans to desire comfort above all else. While we can accept the notion that God sometimes allows suffering for our own good, we would not likely find ourselves DESIRING it. Even in the light of the verse above, we would be more likely to pray for relief than for perseverance in times of struggle. But we are encouraged by New Testament saints to find joy in the **process** because we know that it leads to the completion of our faith.

> *"Consider it pure joy, my brothers and sisters, whenever you face trials of many kinds, because you know that the testing of your faith develops perseverance. Let perseverance finish its work so that you may be mature and complete, not lacking anything."* —James 1:2-4

Suffering for our faith is nothing but an instrument in the hands of God. For by it we gain PERSEVERANCE, which in turn builds in us CHARACTER and generates HOPE. As we have said in past lessons, it is our faith today that produces hope and causes us to see God tomorrow. Look at the verses below:

> *"May the God of **hope** fill you with all joy and peace as you trust in him, so that you may overflow with **hope** by the power of the Holy Spirit."* —Romans 15:13 (emphasis added)

> *"But the eyes of the Lord are on those who fear him, on those whose **hope** is in his unfailing love, to deliver them from death and keep them alive in famine. We wait in **hope** for the Lord; he is our help and our shield. In him our hearts rejoice, for we trust in his holy name. May your unfailing love be with us, Lord, even as we put our **hope** in you."* —Psalm 33:18-22 (emphasis added)

We can see that faith and hope essentially go hand-in-hand. The Bible says that faith is *"confidence in what we hope for"* (Hebrews 11:1). But it is oftentimes hard won. Faith, as we mentioned, requires perseverance in the face of suffering, and the process of building character can be long and discouraging. That is why we find so many verses of encouragement on this point, like the one below:

> *"So do not throw away your confidence; it will be richly rewarded. You need to persevere so that when you have done the will of God, you will receive what he has promised. For, 'In just a very little while, he who is coming will come and will not delay.' And, 'But my righteous one will live by faith. And I take no pleasure in the one who shrinks back.' But we do not belong to those who shrink back and are destroyed, but to those who have faith and are saved."* —Hebrews 10:35-39

And not only do we find encouragement in this process, but we find examples of those who have gone before us. James 5:10-11 talks about *"those who have persevered"* and specifically names Job, whose faith was tested to the extreme. Furthermore, Hebrews 12:3 tells us to consider Jesus *"who endured such opposition from sinners"* so that we will not *"grow weary and lose heart."*

> *"Let us not become weary in doing good, for at the proper time we will reap a harvest if we do not give up."* —Galatians 6:9

Suffering can be a lonely road, but it does not have to be. When we realize the PURPOSE and PLAN of God in it, we can respond in faith at every turn. Romans 12:12 says that we ought to *"Be joyful in hope, patient in affliction, faithful in prayer."* And we can also take comfort that we are not the first to run the race of faith. The verse below tells us that we have a heavenly audience, composed of the men and women of faith who have gone before us, to cheer us on. We are in good company indeed.

> *"Therefore, since we are surrounded by such a great cloud of witnesses, let us throw off everything that hinders and the sin that so easily entangles. And let us run with perseverance the race marked out for us."* —Hebrews 12:1

NOTES:

The Foundation Stones
Faith Toward God

THE TRIAL OF OUR FAITH

> *"Blessed is the man who perseveres under trial because, having stood the test, that person will receive the crown of life that the Lord has promised to those who love him."* —James 1:12

We have touched on the issue of trials a couple of times already, identifying some purposes for God allowing seasons of trial in our lives. Firstly, we have seen that **God will allow testing in order to show us the condition of our hearts.** If we look at Deuteronomy 8:2, we find a classic example of this in the experience of God's people in the desert. Moses wrote, *"Remember how the Lord your God led you all the way in the wilderness these forty years, to humble and test you in order to know what was in your heart, whether or not you would keep his commands."*

And we have also learned that **trials are able to produce perseverance**, which leads to our maturity and completeness. We should consider the struggle worthwhile and even joyful simply because we know that it brings about the perfection of our faith.

> *"Consider it pure joy, my brothers and sisters, whenever you face trials of many kinds, because you know that the testing of your faith develops perseverance. Let perseverance finish its work so that you may be mature and complete, not lacking anything."* —James 1:2-4

But there is still another facet of this issue that we have not yet explored. And that is the **spiritual warfare** that accompanies our trials. Repentance from dead works, as you may remember, is basically a **defense** against the deception of the enemy. It is a turning back toward God in the face of sin. Faith toward God, on the other hand, is an **OFFENSIVE WEAPON** in the hands of a determined Christian.

Most of us would have to admit that our biggest priority is to live comfortable and enjoyable lives. It seems that we are always looking for a peaceful meadow to pop up just around the corner. And, more often than not, we approach our spiritual lives with the same aim. We secretly hope that, as we grow in faith, we will escape the difficulties of life. But it never seems to be the case.

**Faith toward God brings us into warfare.
It teaches us to overcome, not get relief.**

Keep in mind that it is our faith toward God that overcomes the world, and especially the "world" that is within us. We are told in 1 John 5:4 that *"everyone born of God overcomes the world. This is the victory that has overcome the world, even our faith."* When you were born again, you became a kingdom divided within yourself. Your spirit was made alive, but your flesh (sin nature) remained as a dominant force, vying for control. Dismantling our fallen natures requires a complete revolution within, not just a refining of our rough edges. It is the difference between redecorating a room and rebuilding a foundation. And that is what this study is all about. The Bible warns against covering over with "whitewash." For it is the foundation that causes a building to stand or fall in the storms. In Ezekiel 13:13-14, God says, *"I will tear down the wall you have covered with whitewash and will level it to the ground so that its foundation will be laid bare."*

So you see, faith will always cause a conflict **within us**. And the more we grow in faith, the more our flesh will resist it. But there is also a spiritual resistance to our faith that comes from Satan, and it is this matter that we need to focus on today.

"I felt compelled to write and urge you to contend for the faith that was once for all entrusted to God's holy people." —Jude 3

What we need to understand is that we are not contending to OBTAIN (to get God to do something for us). We are fighting to **keep** what has been given to us already. Romans 8:32 tells us, *"He who did not spare his own Son,* *but gave him up for us all—how will he not also, along with him, graciously give us **all things**?"* Remember that we have already been given the riches of God. And Satan knows it well. But as long as WE are unsure of it, he will continue to rob us blind and cause us to go to God as beggars. Have you ever found yourself in this place, pleading with God for what you have allowed the enemy to take from you? Instead, we ought to be going to God in thankfulness, claiming what is ours **even if we do not see it**!! Take a look at the verse below:

> *"However, as it is written: "What no eye has seen, what no ear has heard, and what no human mind has conceived"—the things God has prepared for those who love him—these are the things God has revealed to us by his Spirit. The Spirit searches all things, even the deep things of God. For who knows a person's thoughts except their own spirit within them? In the same way no one knows the thoughts of God except the Spirit of God. What we have received is not the spirit of the world, but the Spirit who is from God, so **that we may understand what God has freely given us**."*
> —1 Corinthians 2:9-12 (emphasis added)

So we can see that the first step in contending for our faith is simply realizing how rich we are. Until we are convinced that we possess the abundance of heaven, we will feel no urge to guard it. And that is why most of us have never stepped up to the plate at all.

THE STRATEGY OF THE ENEMY

It is important to form a **game plan** before a battle. But any athlete could tell you that the key to an unbeatable strategy is to KNOW THE STRATEGY OF YOUR ADVERSARY. And the principal is the same in the spiritual realm. We certainly have a fighting chance with the enemy whenever we stand on the truth, but the best remedy for spiritual attack is to be able to recognize the aim of the attacker. And that is what we want to identify here. In every trial that we go through, there are basically three things that Satan is after. And if he succeeds in robbing us of these, he has essentially stolen our faith.

The Foundation Stones
Faith Toward God

> **The GOODNESS of God**
> **The POWER of God**
> **The PRESENCE of God**

THE GOODNESS OF GOD

The first thing that Satan tries to rob from us is the knowledge of God's goodness. When trials come, he accuses God of withholding His goodness from us. And (to our shame) we often follow along because we are deceived. In our doubt we ask God, "How can You let this happen?" We demand that He prove His heart to us anew before we will trust Him again.

As a matter of fact, sin is a direct result of our deception in this area. When we struggle for self-control, self-improvement, self-sufficiency, self-preservation, etc., we are telling God that we cannot trust Him to take care of us.

> **Sin is simply our effort to supplement what we think are deficiencies in God's goodness.**

> **Faith in God is developing (through Christ) an unshakable confidence in God's absolute goodness and perfect love no matter what we may experience in this life.**

You see, if we let go of the goodness of God, our hope is gone. And that is why Satan hits here every time. We must learn to stand (by faith) on God's character DESPITE our circumstances. And, if we prepare for the attack before it comes, our perspective will be changed and Satan's game plan thwarted. Following are a couple of verses to hold onto:

> *"Taste and see that the Lord is good; blessed is the one who takes refuge in him."* —Psalm 34:8

> *"The Lord is good, a refuge in times of trouble. He cares for those who trust in him."* —Nahum 1:7

Consider two men, Adam and Job, who were confronted with this very deception. Adam, as we all know, ran from God when faced with his sin. He had sided with Eve because he did not know the goodness of God and trust that God could forgive her. And this is the place we find ourselves most often. It is one thing to run to God when we have been victimized by circumstances. But it is an entirely different matter to turn to God in our shame and guilt and cast ourselves on His goodness. It is our confidence in His forgiving heart that draws us to repentance.

Job, on the other hand, suffered trials of the worst kind, and in succession. He was the pawn in a cosmic contest of sorts, and Satan's objective was to prove that Job would curse God were he given enough reason to. But Job stood on the goodness of God even when all else was lost and no explanation was given. And so are we called to stand, even when we do not feel like it or see the purposes of God. We must know that we have tasted God (as in the previous verse) and hold on to that.

THE POWER OF GOD

When we come upon struggles, the enemy encourages us to doubt that God is ABLE and WILLING to deliver us. In this, he is attacking both the power and the heart of God. In the well-known account of Shadrach, Meshach, and Abednego, there is a wonderful example of faith in the face of persecution. The three men of God were about to be thrown into the fiery furnace for refusing to worship an idol. Look at the statement that they made:

The Foundation Stones
Faith Toward God

> "Shadrach, Meshach and Abednego replied to him, 'King Nebuchadnezzar, we do not need to defend ourselves before you in this matter. **If we are thrown into the blazing furnace, the God we serve is able to deliver us from it, and he will deliver us from Your Majesty's hand.** But even if he does not, we want you to know, Your Majesty, that we will not serve your gods or worship the image of gold you have set up.' " —Daniel 3:16-18 (emphasis added)

These men were able to speak boldly and confidently because they KNEW God's power and goodness. You and I live in fear and intimidation simply because we do not know that God is keeping us. And until we do, we will not stand up to the enemy.

In Luke 10:19, Jesus tells us, *"I have given you authority to trample on snakes and scorpions and to overcome all the power of the enemy; nothing will harm you."* But we must first understand the power of God before we appreciate the authority that has been delegated to us. Satan is not afraid of you and me. But he is afraid of God and the power of God working through us.

Most of us, in our pasts, have had our faith challenged. We have walked in doubt because God did not answer, and Satan continually reinforces the lie. The fact is that if we do not stand against the enemy in our lives, he will take advantage every time a trial comes, and GOD WILL LET HIM! We must learn to stand on the truth, and especially when it comes to God's character.

THE PRESENCE OF GOD

> "Do not fear, for I have redeemed you; I have summoned you by name; you are mine. When you pass through the waters, I will be with you; and when you pass through the rivers, they will not sweep over you. When you walk through the fire, you will not be burned; the flames will not set you ablaze." —Isaiah 43:1-2

The Foundation Stones
   Faith Toward God

There are many people today who struggle with the idea that God is ever present and sovereign. We have a hard time understanding how one God can be intimately acquainted with and unceasingly attentive to us individually. But, in reality, God's goodness and power would not be of much help in a trial if it were not for His presence. And so it should be a comfort to know that God walks beside us in our trials, keeping us from harm (as in the previous verse).

But, instead of running toward God, we often find ourselves running away in times of struggle. Maybe we want to be alone, and maybe we are pulling away in resentment from the God who has allowed the situation. But, either way, it is the scheme of the enemy. His priority is to take us out of God's presence so that we are cut off from the Source of Life. And so we must **determine** to come to God, ESPECIALLY when we do not feel like it.

Jesus spoke comforting assurances of His presence to the disciples before leaving this earth. He said, *"surely I am with you always, to the very end of the age"* (Matthew 28:20). But there is more to God's presence than simple companionship. With it comes REST to our souls, as God promised Moses:

> *"The Lord replied, 'My Presence will go with you, and I will give you rest.'"* —Exodus 33:14

If there is one thing that makes the difference in these times, it is our perspective. Yes, God WILL allow trials to come. Storms roll through the lives of the righteous and the wicked alike. And we can also count on the inevitable struggle when we respond in faith. But God's aim is NOT to see how much we can stand. He wants to bring us to a place of security in Him. It is a **fixed heart** that He desires for you and me, one that is steadfast and immovable because it is grounded in the immovable love of God.

> *"They will have **no fear** of bad news; their hearts are **steadfast**, **trusting** in the Lord. Their hearts are **secure**, they will have no fear; in the end they will look in triumph on their foes."*
> —Psalm 112:7-8 (emphasis added)

The Foundation Stones
Faith Toward God

EXAMINING OUR FAITH

"Examine yourselves to see whether you are in the faith; test yourselves. Do you not realize that Christ Jesus is in you—unless, of course, you fail the test?" —2 Corinthians 13:5

As we come to the end of our discussion on Faith Toward God, we need to be reminded of the importance of this spiritual element. Hebrews 11:6 tells us that *"without faith it is **impossible** to please God, because anyone who comes to him must believe that he exists and that he rewards those who earnestly seek him."* And it is for this reason that we are called to EXAMINE our faith. We must test ourselves in order to know that we are truly "in the faith" as evidence that Christ Jesus lives inside of us. If we find that we are not, we may legitimately wonder about the authenticity of our relationship with Him.

- **Examine** – Investigate, inspect, survey, probe, scrutinize, dissect, interrogate, question, audit and review[4]

When examining your faith, keep in mind what faith is really all about. Faith is always active, always moving forward, always pressing in to God. It is NOT as simple as saying, "Yes, I believe." If we really BELIEVE, we will move in faith. True faith already possesses what God has said. While someone who is walking in unbelief may quote Scriptures and even claim them, FAITH **ACTS** ON THEM.

Believing is ACTING on the Word.

Look at the points of examination starting on the next page and identify your position. But don't stop there. If you find that you are not where you should be, then start walking by faith NOW. The journey of faith may be miles long, but the first step is worth just as much in God's eyes as the last.

WE ARE CALLED TO:

Walk By Faith

A walk of faith is more than just a profession of our belief in God. It is to trust in and be motivated by what we cannot see with our eyes (the eternal). It is a deliberate stepping out into the covering of God's promises with nothing else to lean on. If we are truly walking by faith, we are painfully yet joyfully aware of our dependence on God with every step we take.

> *"For we **walk by faith**, not by sight."*
> —2 Corinthians 5:7 (NKJV) (emphasis added)

> *"[L]et us run with perseverance the race marked out for us, fixing our eyes on Jesus, the pioneer and perfecter of faith"* —Hebrews 12:1-2

Live By Faith

A life of faith is easily recognized by the newness of outlook and lifestyle that it produces. The Word of God tells us that the RIGHTEOUS will live by faith. Until we entrust ourselves to the grace and provision of God, we will never be justified in God's eyes. Faith is actively trusting that what HE HAS ALREADY DONE is enough for us, to cover, protect, forgive, provide, and redeem. We will know that we are living by faith when we are continually staking our lives on the grace of God.

> *"For in the gospel the righteousness of God is revealed—a righteousness that is by faith from first to last, just as it is written: 'The righteous will **live by faith**.'"* —Romans 1:17 (emphasis added)

> *"Clearly no one is justified before God by the law because, 'The righteous will **live by faith**.'"* —Galatians 3:11 (emphasis added)

Overcome By Faith

God's Word tells us that it is our faith that overcomes the world. If we struggle with feeling defeated, then we can safely assume that we are not moving by faith. For true faith believes that we have the victory in Christ apart from all that we experience. It is a confidence that rises above the circumstances of our lives and causes us to overcome daily.

> *"[F]or everyone born of God **overcomes** the world. This is the victory that has **overcome** the world, even our faith. Who is it that **overcomes** the world? Only the one who believes that Jesus is the Son of God."*
> —1 John 5:4-5 (emphasis added)

> *"But thanks be to God, who always leads us as captives in Christ's triumphal procession."* —2 Corinthians 2:14

Stand By Faith

Whether we are speaking of walking or living or overcoming by faith, we can be sure of one common denominator. To operate by faith is to simply stand the ground that God has given us. Ephesians 6:13 encourages us to *"put on the full armor of God, so that when the day of evil comes, you may be able to stand your ground, and after you have done everything, to stand."* We must firmly plant our hearts on the truth of God's Word so that nothing can move us. He who stands by faith is grounded in the stability and unshakable peace of Christ.

The Foundation Stones
Faith Toward God

> *"because it is **by faith you stand firm**"*
> —2 Corinthians 1:24 (emphasis added)

> *"[C]ontinue in your faith, established and firm, and do not move from the hope held out in the gospel."* —Colossians 1:23

In the book of Philemon verse 6 (NKJV), we find a wonderful tool for the building up of our faith. We are told that *"the sharing of your faith may become effective **by the acknowledgment of every good thing which is in you in Christ Jesus.**"* We need to constantly recognize the workings of God within us. And, by doing so, our eyes will be opened to the ways of God and our faith built up. Take, for instance, the simple statements below. Affirm these truths as they apply specifically to you, and expect to see your faith "become effective."

THINGS TO AFFIRM

God is who He says He is.
I am who God says I am.

God can do what He says He can do.
I can do what God says I can do.

God has what He says He has.
I have what God says I have.

The Foundation Stones
Faith Toward God

Keep in mind that our faith is a witness to the world that it overcomes. As Christians, our unbelief is a betrayal of God's faithfulness, but our faith is the greatest testimony to it. If for no other reason, choose to stand in faith simply because God is worthy of your trust.

> *"Let us hold unswervingly to the hope we profess, for he who promised is faithful."* —Hebrews 10:23

NOTES:

The Foundation Stones
Faith Toward God

NOTES:

DOCTRINE OF BAPTISMS

DOCTRINE OF BAPTISMS

INTRODUCTION

The third of the six foundation stones found in Hebrews 5:12 through 6:2 is called the **"Doctrine of Baptisms."** And, while many of us are familiar with the practice of water baptism, there is much more to understand about the concept of baptism, as well as several more types of baptism to explore. Below is a list of the baptisms, all of which we are going to touch on in this teaching:

> **Baptism into Repentance**
>
> **Baptism into Water**
>
> **Baptism into the Holy Ghost**
>
> **Baptism into Fire**
>
> **Baptism into His Body**
>
> **Baptism into Suffering**
>
> **Baptism into the Cloud**

Before we begin to address the baptisms specifically, let's take a look at the basic elements of baptism. At some point in our Christian experience, many of us have been baptized with water. Traditionally, in a water baptism, an individual makes a profession of faith and is then submersed in water (figuratively or literally). Ideally, this is done with the understanding that it is a symbol of the death and resurrection of Christ. Even so, the public practice of water baptism is nothing more than a shadow. Just as we have said before, Christian "rituals" are meant to point us to the substance (or reality) in Christ Himself, and baptism is no exception. If you have believed baptism to be little more than a ceremonial act, you are certainly not alone. But be assured that there is more to it.

Below are the three elements that make up baptism:

> 1. **Identification** – with something or someone specific
> 2. **Transition** – in perspective or position
> 3. **Newness** – of thinking or direction

The first point of baptism, **identification**, has much to do with our discussions in the previous sections. It is the revelation of our identity in Christ. This is where Satan attacks the most, simply because the other two elements follow naturally from it. Each new facet of **identification** ushered in by a baptism brings about a **transition** in perspective and **newness** of mind. This should be our daily experience as we venture deeper into relationship with Him. It is how we are transformed into the image of Christ.

Even the baptism of Jesus by John (recorded in Matthew 3:13-17) included these elements. We can be sure that Jesus never needed redirection or clarification on His identity as we do, for Jesus was God incarnate. He was actually baptized for *our* benefit in order to:

Identify with unrighteous man
Begin the **transition** into His teaching ministry
And usher in a **newness** of direction in the display of His power.

Jesus (being God) experienced baptism while on this earth so that He could identify with you and me. In doing so, He has enabled us to identify with and be transformed by the things of God.

The Foundation Stones
Doctrine of Baptisms

- **Baptize** – to overwhelm, cover over completely, submerge, completely put into.[5]

Baptism is not an isolated event or a one-time experience. It is a lifestyle. We enter spiritually into a baptism as a diver into water. There is a point in time at which we knowingly enter in (comparable to the water surface), and, as water swallows up a person, so we are engulfed and enveloped in the baptism. As we continue in it, we grow ever deeper in its understanding and practical application. And, just as in diving, there comes a point of no return, beyond which we can no longer save ourselves. Baptism brings us into the depths of relationship that God desires for us, but it requires self-abandonment and complete trust in Him.

NOTES:

BAPTISM INTO REPENTANCE

"I baptize you with water for repentance"
—Matthew 3:11

The **Baptism into Repentance** actually begins at the point of our salvation. The Holy Spirit first convicts us of sin and brings us to repentance that we may accept the atonement of Christ for ourselves. And so we can logically conclude that all of us, assuming that we have walked through the salvation experience, have already entered into this baptism. The matter at hand is this: Have we continued any deeper or simply remained at the surface? If we are truly growing in the Lord, we will find ourselves repenting more than ever. We will never grow out of repentance. Rather, repentance must become a lifestyle for us.

Repentance, as you may remember, is a turning from sin to God. The Bible speaks of two kinds of sorrow, one that leads to repentance and life and the other that leads to death.

> *"Godly sorrow brings repentance that leads to salvation and leaves no regret, but worldly sorrow brings death."* —2 Corinthians 7:10

The "worldly sorrow" is a regret that non-Christians cannot escape simply because the world offers no relief from shame and guilt. "Godly sorrow," on the other hand, is what draws us to repentance. Where worldly sorrow brings regret due to the consequences of sin, Godly sorrow results in a change of heart and recognition of our sinful condition apart from God. The difference is that, when we turn to God, we find the remedy for sin in the blood of Christ. We are, in a sense, exchanging our sin-stained garments for the righteousness of Christ. We can return to God because we know that His love and grace are enough to cover us.

> " 'Even now,' declares the Lord, 'return to me with all your heart, with fasting and weeping and mourning.' Rend your heart and not your garments. Return to the Lord your God, for he is gracious and compassionate, slow to anger and abounding in love, and he relents from sending calamity." —Joel 2:12-13

The Baptism into Repentance has a very specific purpose in our lives. It is not just for correction or redirection, although it certainly may serve in these capacities as well. By walking consistently in repentance, we are actually dying to ourselves in order to make room for God. You see, our sin will remain on the throne of our hearts as long as we allow it to. By turning, in obedience, from sin and to God, we are essentially preparing that place for Him.

The purpose of the Baptism into Repentance is to prepare a place for God in our hearts.

> "This is what the Lord says: 'Heaven is my throne, and the earth is my footstool. Where is the house you will build for me? Where will my resting place be?' " —Isaiah 66:1

Let us take a look at the three elements of baptism as they apply to the Baptism into Repentance.

IDENTIFICATION with the Holiness of God

The Baptism into Repentance begins with the identification with God's Holiness. When God shines His Holy light into our lives, what we see is our wretched condition apart from Him. And it is the awareness of our great need that draws us to repentance. If we desire to see God, He will show Himself to us. But we must first **know** repentance simply because we cannot stand before the holiness of God on our own merit. It is only by the gift of righteousness, which is ours through repentance, that we are made acceptable in God's eyes.

> *"For if, by the trespass of the one man, death reigned through that one man, how much more will those who receive God's abundant provision of grace and of the gift of righteousness reign in life through the one man, Jesus Christ!"* —Romans 5:17

We cannot reconcile ourselves or our past to God. We cannot now and never will measure up to the Holiness of God. We have no moves but to repent. And that is why repentance will always grow as we grow in closeness to God. Simply said, we are NEVER going to get **better**. We can only hope to become more and more aware of our desperate need for Him.

A CHANGE in perspective and of the heart (repentance)

The change that results from the Baptism into Repentance is one of the heart, but it is made known by the actions (or "fruit") it produces. In Matthew 3:8, John the Baptist (who preached a message of repentance) warned the Pharisees and the Sadducees to *"Produce fruit in keeping with repentance."* And the fruit that he was speaking of is an outward turning from sin and a hunger for purity and righteousness. These are SIGNS that God is changing the desires and motivations of a heart.

The NEWNESS of a heart broken and prepared for Him

In Matthew 3:6, we are told that the people John was baptizing were *"Confessing their sins."* Now, it may seem an insignificant point, but there is actually a great deal of meaning behind this statement. Those who were desiring baptism were **humble and broken** to the point where their shame and guilt were no longer worth hiding. This is the newness that comes with the Baptism of Repentance. When we have truly walked in repentance and have been **undone** by the Holiness of God, our pride is no longer a stumbling block. This is the heart that God does not despise (see Psalm 51:17). It is a clean vessel, a heart prepared for Him.

The Foundation Stones
  Doctrine of Baptisms

John the Baptist was said to have come in the spirit of Elijah and Isaiah (see Luke 1:17 and John 1:19-28) because he preached the message of repentance. John was called to prepare the way for Christ on this earth just as the repentance he spoke of prepares the way for Him in our hearts. Luke 1:16-17 tells us that John was sent *"... to turn the hearts of the ... disobedient to the wisdom of the righteous—to make ready a people prepared for the Lord."* John quoted a verse from the book of Isaiah, which gives us insight into the newness that God desires to bring you and me through the Baptism into Repentance. Let's take a look at it.

> *"The voice of one crying in the wilderness: 'Prepare the way of the Lord; make straight in the desert a highway for our God. Every valley shall be exalted and every mountain and hill brought low; the crooked places shall be made straight and the rough places smooth; the glory of the Lord shall be revealed, and all flesh shall see it together; for the mouth of the Lord has spoken.'"* —Isaiah 40:3-5 NKJV

John the Baptist is viewed in this verse as the one calling people to repentance, calling them to prepare a place in their hearts for the Lord and to "make straight" His way. Those who do not continue in the Baptism into Repentance often find themselves walking in spiritual circles just as the disobedient Israelites wandered in the wilderness. Repentance is our **straight line** to God, meaning that it is the shortest distance between where we are now and where God desires us to be. The Baptism into Repentance "makes straight" a path for God.

We find in verse 3 of the Isaiah 40 passage that God desires to both raise up the "valleys" and to bring low the "mountains" in us. Ephesians 2:6 tells us that *"... God raised us up with Christ and seated us with him in the heavenly realms ..."* God has already raised us up to the level of His own Son. It is only our pride that keeps us from accepting the grace to be all that God has called us to be. After all, we are not just the sum of our experiences, **we are who God says we are!**

"But by the grace of God I am what I am, and His grace toward me was not in vain" —1 Corinthians 15:10 NKJV

On the same token, repentance also brings about a humility (or brokenness) that draws us to the cross. It is through this that God is able to lift us up. And so the two work hand-in-hand, complimenting one another. Take a look at just a few of the verses that speak about God's response to a humble heart:

*"Lord, You have heard the desire of the **humble**; You will prepare their heart; You will cause Your ear to hear"*
—Psalm 10:17 (NKJV) (emphasis added)

*"The highway of the upright is to depart from evil; he who keeps his way preserves his soul. Pride goes before destruction and a haughty spirit before a fall. Better to be of a **humble** spirit with the lowly than to divide the spoil with the proud."*
—Proverbs 16:17-19 (NKJV) (emphasis added)

*"A man's pride will bring him low, but the **humble** in spirit will retain honor."* —Proverbs 29:23 (NKJV) (emphasis added)

*"I dwell in the high and holy place, with him who has a **contrite** and **humble** spirit, to revive the spirit of the **humble**, and to revive the heart of the **contrite** ones."* —Isaiah 57:15 (NKJV) (emphasis added)

*"Therefore, whoever **humbles** himself as this little child is the greatest in the kingdom of heaven."* —Matthew 18:4 NKJV (emphasis added)

*"All of you, clothe yourselves with **humility** toward one another, because, 'God opposes the proud but shows favor to the **humble**.' **Humble** yourselves, therefore, under God's mighty hand, that he may lift you up in due time."* —1 Peter 5:5-6 (emphasis added)

The Foundation Stones
   Doctrine of Baptisms

> *"**Humble** yourselves before the Lord, and he will lift you up."*
> —James 4:10 (emphasis added)

> *"He has shown you, O Man, what is good; and what does the Lord require of you but to do justly, to love mercy, and to walk **humbly** with your God?"* —Micah 6:8 NKJV (emphasis added)

Continuing on in the Isaiah 40 passage, verse 4 also tells us that *"the rough ground shall become level, the rugged places a plain."* Through the Baptism into Repentance the "rough ground" of our sin nature is broken under God's hand. The result is the leveling of our paths and the sharpening of our characters.

> *" As iron sharpens iron, so one man sharpens another. "*
> —Proverbs 27:17

> *"I will lead them beside streams of water on a level path where they will not stumble"* —Jeremiah 31:9

Isaiah 40, verse 5 tells us further: *"And the glory of the Lord will be revealed."* This is the result of the Baptism into Repentance. It is a glory that "all mankind together" will see because it is a work of God.

> *"In the same way, let your light shine before others, that they may see your good deeds and glorify your Father in heaven."* —Matthew 5:16

> *"And we all, who with unveiled faces contemplate the Lord's glory, are being transformed into his image with ever-increasing glory, which comes from the Lord, who is the Spirit."* —2 Corinthians 3:18

BROKENNESS—The Fruit Of Repentance

Walking in the Baptism into Repentance, as we have said, prepares a place for God in our hearts. But it also creates a **desire** for God within us, which we cannot otherwise muster up. When we turned to God for salvation (which marked our first step in this baptism), it was due to the CONVICTION of the Holy Spirit. His call to repentance was our first experience in **hearing** and **responding** to God. But it does not stop there. **Walking in repentance actually enables us to hear and draw close to God on a daily basis.** If we say that repentance should be a lifestyle for us, then we must assume that the same is true for hearing God. Many of us believe that hearing God is for the spiritual giants of our time. But the truth is that being led by the Holy Spirit is nothing more than **normal Christianity**. If we do not hear God speaking to us currently, we have good reason to be concerned. It is a sign that we have stopped yielding to (and possibly even recognizing) the conviction of the Holy Spirit within us. Our unwillingness to repent will stand in the way of an intimate acquaintance with our Lord because it is repentance that creates within us a passion for God and a hunger for His presence in our lives.

> The repentant heart has such a passion for God's presence that it recognizes immediately when it is gone and does whatever it takes to restore it.

Surely we can each examine ourselves to know whether or not we experience the unhindered walk with God that repentance brings. If we have never been taught that an intimate relationship with the Lord is the basis of Christianity, then this may be the moment of realizing that something (namely, God's presence) is indeed missing. But most of us do not have to be persuaded that we are left wanting in this area. And there is a great deal of evidence in each of our lives to prove that the lack exists. For the Baptism into Repentance produces the fruit of BROKENNESS. And so the **absence** of brokenness is actually a testimony to our unrepentant hearts.

The Foundation Stones
  Doctrine of Baptisms

Have you ever wondered at the types of people Jesus seemed to gravitate to? We might have expected that He would embrace the scholarly and respected religious leaders of the day. But He did not. Jesus' favorite people were children, as well as the childlike (see Luke 10:21). Now what does that tell us? It tells us that God is not interested so much in our education, our maturity, or our experience as He is in the condition of our hearts.

> *"These are the ones I look on with favor: those who are humble and contrite in spirit, and who tremble at my word."* —Isaiah 66:2

Luke 18:9-14 records The Parable of the Pharisee and the Tax Collector as told by Jesus. It speaks of two men, one a religious leader and the other a despised tax collector, who went to the temple to pray. The Pharisee started his prayer by saying, *"God, I thank you that I am not like other people—robbers, evildoers, adulterers—or even like this tax collector."* The tax collector, on the other hand, *"stood at a distance. He would not even look up to heaven, but beat his breast and said, 'God, have mercy on me, a sinner.'"* Jesus told the crowd that the tax collector and not the Pharisee *"went home justified before God."* Why? Was it because he said the magic words? Not exactly. But our words often reveal the condition of our hearts (as was the case with these two men), and God responds to brokenness.

Self-centeredness is at the core of the unrepentant heart, and so it is a telltale measure of our brokenness. In order to walk in the Baptism into Repentance we must consistently come to the Cross and choose freely to lay down our own self-interests. It is surrendering to the will of God and denying ourselves our "rights." After all, our lives are no longer our own if we have asked Him to be our Lord.

God's desire is that we are BROKEN in defense of ourselves. And not only that, we ought to be asking Him to expose our sin in love. If this sounds unrealistic, then we may be getting a glimpse into our own hearts. You see our biggest enemy, when it comes to **experiencing** God, is not Satan but OURSELVES! It is only our **pride** and **lack of repentance** that stands in the way of the reality of God's presence. The Bible tells us that nothing in all creation *"will be able to separate us from the love of God that is in Christ Jesus our Lord"* (Romans 8:35-39)—that is, **as long as WE do not separate ourselves from Him.**

This leads us to the first of **three indicators of brokenness** in our lives:

I.
A willingness to deal with known sin in our lives, AND a desire for God to reveal any sin we are not yet aware of.

Look at how David, the king of Israel and a "man after God's own heart," responded to God in his brokenness:

"Search me, O God, and know my heart; test me and know my anxious thoughts. See if there is any offensive way in me, and lead me in the way everlasting." —Psalm 139:23-24

Anything less than abandonment to the searching, testing, and leading of God's Spirit will prove to be a barrier in our relationships with Him.

II.
The ability to receive God's Word, not for knowledge, but for life.

The Bible warns us, *"Do not merely listen to the word, and so deceive yourselves. Do what it says"* (James 1:22). The majority of Christians today are deceived in regards to the Word of God. We approach the Bible all too often as we would a piece of classic literature. It has become to us a source of information when it should be OUR LIVES! God did not spend thousands of years inspiring and preserving His Word for our intellectual pleasure. If we are not **applying** the truth to our lives deliberately and consistently, then we too are deceiving ourselves.

> *"All Scripture is God-breathed and is useful for **teaching, rebuking, correcting,** and **training in righteousness.**"*
> —2 Timothy 3:16-17 (emphasis added)

The purposes of the Scripture can be broken down into these four categories (as specified in the verse above): It was given to **teach** (by doctrine), **rebuke** (reproof over known sin), **correct** (convict of sin), and **train** (instruct). But our hearts will not receive these except by brokenness.

**III.
A heart to follow the instruction of the Word of God and build on the truths received.**

This element of brokenness is a natural extension of the first two. When we have begun to deal with sin in our lives and receive the Word of God as an instrument of change, our hearts will be easily moved in obedience to the truths we have held to.

In addition to the spiritual evidences of a broken and contrite heart, there is a practical outworking of brokenness that becomes apparent in our interaction with others. Brokenness must first be toward God, but it automatically carries over into our interpersonal relationships. It is not that both are **required**, but rather that they naturally occur together. Consequently, we cannot be walking in the Baptism into Repentance if we are REACTING to those around us.

People of today have been swept away in the fight for their rights. We often join the ranks in retaliation without realizing that God actually uses people as instruments to bring brokenness into our lives. When we react to someone, we are engaging in a conflict of wills. A broken and repentant heart, however, will refer to God first and then respond to others in meekness (power under control). Self-control, after all, is fruit of the Holy Spirit.

Think about this for a minute. When you mess up, does your passion for God draw you back to repentance quickly? If we are trying to keep ourselves from retaliating out of our love for others, we will fail every time. Only the constraining love of God is strong enough. But do not misunderstand; the Holy Spirit does not MAKE us humble. He enables us to humble ourselves.

The practical result of brokenness is illustrated vividly in the life of Jesus. Look, for example, at the words Jesus spoke to His disciples:

> *"Instead, the greatest among you should be like the youngest, and the one who rules like the one who serves. For who is greater, the one who is at the table or the one who serves? Is it not the one who is at the table? But I am among you as one who serves."* —Luke 22:24-27

The Son of God, under whose feet all things in heaven and earth have been placed, came to Earth in the form of a ... **SERVANT?** There is no doubt that Jesus knew the power and authority that had been given to Him, and His natural response was to serve the same men who would betray, abandon, and sentence Him to death. Philippians 2:7 (NKJV) tells us that He *"made himself of no reputation, taking the form of a bondservant, and coming in the likeness of men."*

And where does that leave us, those who are co-heirs with Christ? Can there be a higher calling than the humility and brokenness of a servant if that was the priority of Jesus? The truth is that all of us, believers and nonbelievers alike, are slaves to one of two things—SIN or RIGHTEOUSNESS. The enemy is out to break our wills, but God's design is that our wills are submitted to Him in love. We are called to be bondservants (love-slaves) to both God and others. The only alternative is bondage to the god of this world.

Jesus demonstrated His love for the disciples by washing their feet at the Last Supper. John 13:1 tells us that, *"Having loved his own who were in the*

The Foundation Stones
Doctrine of Baptisms

world, he loved them to the end." And so we are also to serve God and others as a demonstration of love. Brokenness always materializes in the act of serving, and so it is the heart condition that God desires.

Look at just a few of the verses that speak of servanthood:

> *"Not so with you. Instead, whoever wants to become great among you must be your servant, and whoever wants to be first must be your slave."* —Matthew 20:26-27

> *"You, my brothers and sisters, were called to be free. But do not use your freedom to indulge the flesh; rather, serve one another humbly in love."* —Galatians 5:13

> *"[J]ust as the Son of Man did not come to be served, but to serve, and to give his life as a ransom for many."* —Matthew 20:28

> *"Do nothing out of selfish ambition or vain conceit. Rather, in humility value others above yourselves, not looking to your own interests but each of you to the interests of the others."* —Philippians 2:3-4

"In what, then, does abiding in Christ consist? ... It consists, first, in a willingness to repent quickly whenever sin comes in ... Second, it means continually seeing Jesus as the Vine, living and acting for others in the power of His limitless resources. Then there is the continuous faith that reckons on its union with this precious Vine. Such faith does not ask to be united to Him, but takes its stand that it is united already, and praises Him for His life made ours. With that there is the brokenness that continually yields its rights and interests to Jesus ... Lastly, there is the pouring out of love to others, not in word only but in deed ..."

—"We Would See Jesus" (Roy and Revel Hession)[2]

NOTES:

The Foundation Stones
Doctrine of Baptisms

BAPTISM INTO WATER

> *"[A]ll of us who were baptized into Christ Jesus were baptized into his death"* —Romans 6:3-4

Water baptism is a common practice in Christian churches today, and most Christians would claim to have a basic understanding of this baptism even if they are not familiar with the other six. However, do not be too quick to assume that this is true because, as you may remember, the practice of water baptism is only a shadow of the reality of the Baptism into Water. If, therefore, we have been baptized in the literal sense but have not experienced the true baptism—that is, the identification, change, and newness in Christ—then we are kidding ourselves. And the fact is that the primary reason that Christians struggle in their walk is a lack of understanding of this particular doctrine. For the Baptism into Water brings us to identification with Christ's death, burial, and resurrection, which is the basis of our Salvation. Without this, our faith is a lie and we are hopelessly lost in our sins.

Ephesians 4:11-15 challenges believers to enter into their identity in Christ. It tells us that God's purpose is that *"the body of Christ may be built up until we all reach unity in the faith and in the knowledge of the Son of God and become mature, attaining to the whole measure of the fullness of Christ."* If this is the case, then we have to wonder why many Christians are so preoccupied and defeated spiritually. If Satan is a lesser force than God, why are we not experiencing victory? It is because we do not understand and use the power that has been given to us, the power that results from genuine identification with the death, burial, and resurrection of Christ.

IDENTIFICATION
with the death, burial, and resurrection of Jesus

> *"Your attitude should be the same as that of Christ Jesus: Who, being in very nature God, did not consider equality with God something to be grasped, but made himself nothing, taking the very nature of a*

servant, being made in human likeness. And being found in appearance as a man, he humbled himself and became obedient to death—even death on a cross!" —Philippians 2:5-8

Jesus came to this earth in order to identify with us in the flesh. It is interesting to note that He called himself the "Son of Man" and not the "Son of God" while He was among us (see Luke 19:10, Matthew 20:28, and John 5:26-27 for examples). As a matter of fact, He used this title **thirty-two** times in Matthew alone. Why did He feel the need to do this? After all, He was fully God and had every right to claim it. His purpose for coming in the form of man was to EXCHANGE identities with you and me, to take on our sin and MAKE US the righteousness of God.

I know you have probably heard the phrase a hundred times or more, but stop for a minute to think about it. Christ died on the cross as your **substitute**. And, not only that, YOU DIED WITH HIM! Do you realize that God put you and me in Christ at the cross? In God's mind, WE died, we were buried, and we were raised to life with Jesus! Christ overcame so that we could also overcome. It is the power of substitution in its grandest form. Charles Spurgeon had this to say about it:

> **"In one word, the great pillar of the Christian's hope is substitution. ... Men cannot bear substitution. They gnash their teeth at the thought of the Lamb of God bearing the sin of man. But we, who know by experience the preciousness of this truth, will proclaim it in defiance of them confidently and unceasingly. We will neither dilute it nor change it, nor fritter it away in any shape or fashion. ... We cannot, dare not, give it up, for it is our life."**
> **—Charles Spurgeon**

This is a reality that we cannot afford to live without. God finds our identity in Christ alone. But we are so quick to believe the lies of the enemy and search for our identity elsewhere. When we stand before Him, He sees nothing but the righteousness of Christ! And, when we truly understand this, it will set us free. Pay attention to the echoes of triumph in the verse below:

> *"[A]nd in Christ you have been brought to fullness. He is the head over every power and authority ... having been buried with him in baptism, in which you were also raised with him through your faith in the working of God, who raised him from the dead. When you were dead in your sins and in the uncircumcision of your flesh, God made you alive with Christ. He forgave us all our sins, having canceled the charge of our legal indebtedness, which stood against us and condemned us; he has taken it away, nailing it to the cross. And having disarmed the powers and authorities, he made a public spectacle of them, triumphing over them by the cross."* —Colossians 2:10-15

What is our role in all of this? It is simply to step into the reality of what Jesus has done and identify so deeply with Him that **WE** no longer live. As Paul said in Galatians 2:20, *"I have been crucified with Christ and I no longer live, but Christ lives in me. The life I now live in the body, I live by faith in the Son of God, who loved me and gave himself for me."* This is the change that results from identification with the Son of God. It is the **burial** of **MY** life in light of the death of Christ as my substitute.

A CHANGE in lifestyle—actively dying to myself

And what is the newness that results? The newness is the power of Christ's resurrection at work in you and me.

The NEWNESS of resurrection power and life in Christ

It is indeed a critical process to walk through. In fact, it is the core of our Christian faith, whether we realize it or not. Without the power that comes from our identification with the work of Christ, Christianity is a joke. And

The Foundation Stones
Doctrine of Baptisms

so it seems to many people simply because they find no power within themselves to overcome sin. We must understand that we were never designed to walk the Christian walk without the power of the resurrection. It cannot be done. It is unrealistic to believe that we are simply called to be *imitators* of Christ. We have been called to be **found in** and to **live through** Christ Jesus.

What do you suppose is the stumbling block for most Christians at this point? We often conclude that if our minds cannot understand something, then it cannot be true. We reject the truth based on our intellect, and we dare God to prove it to us. What we need to realize is that truth can be defined in two different ways. We are accustomed to operating on a **subjective** level, relying on our feelings and personal experiences to dictate our beliefs. But there is an **objective** truth that exists apart from our acceptance of it. For example, we can believe with all of our hearts that $2+2=5$, but all of our sincerity amounts to nothing in the light of the objective truth. Such is the case with the things of God. Remember that believing a lie does not make it the truth, no matter how our feelings or experiences seem to back it up.

- **Objective Truth** – factual, solid, existing apart from experience or feelings

- **Subjective Truth** – of or resulting from one's feelings or thinking rather than just plain fact

> "What shall we say, then? Shall we go on sinning so that grace may increase? By no means! We are those who have died to sin; how can we live in it any longer? **Or don't you know that all of us who were baptized into Christ Jesus were baptized into his death? We were therefore buried with him through baptism into death in order that, just as Christ was raised from the dead through the glory of the Father, we too may live a new life.** For if we have been united with him in a death like his, we will certainly also be united with him in a resurrection like his. For we know that our old self was crucified

with him so that the body ruled by sin might be done away with, that we should no longer be slaves to sin—because anyone who has died has been set free from sin. Now if we died with Christ, we believe that we will also live with him." —Romans 6:1-8 (emphasis added)

There are three ASPECTS OF THE CROSS that we need to understand before stepping into this baptism:

THE OBJECTIVE FACT

We have utterly and entirely died in Christ as our substitute, regardless of our feelings, circumstances, or actions.

This is the basis of our Salvation. If this has not happened, then we have no hope. The verse above uses a word for "die" that actually means *to be consummated in a finished act*. We must believe it simply because God said it. **It is not until we stand in faith on the objective truth of God's Word that it becomes our experience.** Think about it for a minute. Is this not also true about the lies of the enemy? When we believe a lie, it becomes subjective (it works out in our experience).

 The Father's desire is for all to identify with His Son. We are never told to try to put ourselves to death, but to reckon on the fact.

THE SUBJECTIVE OUTWORKING

The reality of the cross comes through putting to death (burying, in a sense) the works of the flesh daily.

Galatians 5:24 tells us: *"Those who belong to Christ Jesus have crucified the flesh with its passions and desires."* Our death in Christ actually freed us from our bondage to sin. Romans 7:1-6 explains that sin only has authority over us as long as we are alive. In the work of the cross, we have died to sin in order that we might belong to Christ. It is comparable to the nullification of one marriage by death of a spouse (our death to sin) in order that a new marriage (to Christ) is possible. We have been assured that God has closed this door by death. But what happens is that sin, the enemy, comes back to claim its right to our lives, and **we** open the door to it! We are so comfortable with the lies and unsure of Jesus' love that we pass by the work of the cross entirely. The Bible encourages us to *"count yourselves dead to sin but alive to God in Christ Jesus"* (Romans 6:11). That means that when the lies come in along with the temptation to sin, we must choose to believe that we have died to it.

> *"For if you live according to the flesh, you will die; but if by the Spirit you put to death the misdeeds of the body, you will live."*
> —Romans 8:13

"The Radium of the Cross"

Let's look at an analogy that may put this into perspective for us. Radium is a radioactive material that has the power to kill by simple exposure. If a piece of radium were placed in the center of a room filled with people, nobody would feel or understand the effects of the substance at the time. But the exposure would remain with each person for the rest of his or her life, slowly and undetectably working death into the body. In a sense, this is the role of the cross within each of us. It has the power to put us (our sinful nature) to death without an ounce of our energy. We need not even understand the workings of the cross. We must simply count on its work, for it can never be separated from Salvation. If we do not see this happening within us over a period of time, we can be sure that we have settled for a shadow in place of true Life.

The Foundation Stones
  Doctrine of Baptisms

THE POWER

Through the cross, the life of Christ is imparted to us in power to overcome the world, the flesh, and the devil.

*"I want to know Christ—yes, to know the **power of his resurrection** and participation in his sufferings, becoming like him in his death, and so, somehow, attaining to the resurrection from the dead."*
—Philippians 3:10-11 (emphasis added)

It is safe to say that most Christians never experience the power of the resurrection in their lives simply because they are not believing the truth. With our natural minds we can see only the grave, and so we save ourselves from the work of the cross time and again. But it is only in the grave that we find the presence of God and receive the promise of resurrection and life. We are called to identify daily with the death of Christ in order that resurrection life may be imparted to us. Paul, for instance, said, *"We always carry around in our body the death of Jesus, so that the life of Jesus may also be revealed in our body. For we who are alive are always being given over to death for Jesus' sake, so that his life may also be revealed in our mortal body."* (2 Corinthians 4:10-11)

The truth is that, ultimately, a Christian cannot escape the death of the cross. We have no power without it (see 1 Corinthians 15). But the cross is a stumbling block and foolishness to the lost mind. We must ask God for personal revelation of this. For it is only by revelation that we can go from the **objective truth** of the cross to the **subjective outworking** and **power**. And we *must* go through these three steps, or it is a lie.

The work of the cross in our lives is complete and dramatic. We are told in 2 Corinthians 5:17 (NKJV) that *"if anyone is in Christ, he is a new creation; old things have passed away; behold, all things have become new."* God has ALREADY placed our identity in Christ. It is only our unbelief that stands in the way of experiencing it. We have been set free from the talons of this world and commissioned to a newness of life in the Spirit.

The Foundation Stones
Doctrine of Baptisms

"But now, by dying to what once bound us, we have been released from the law so that we serve in the new way of the Spirit, and not in the old way of the written code." —Romans 7:6

THE WORLDLY CIRCLE OF EVENTS

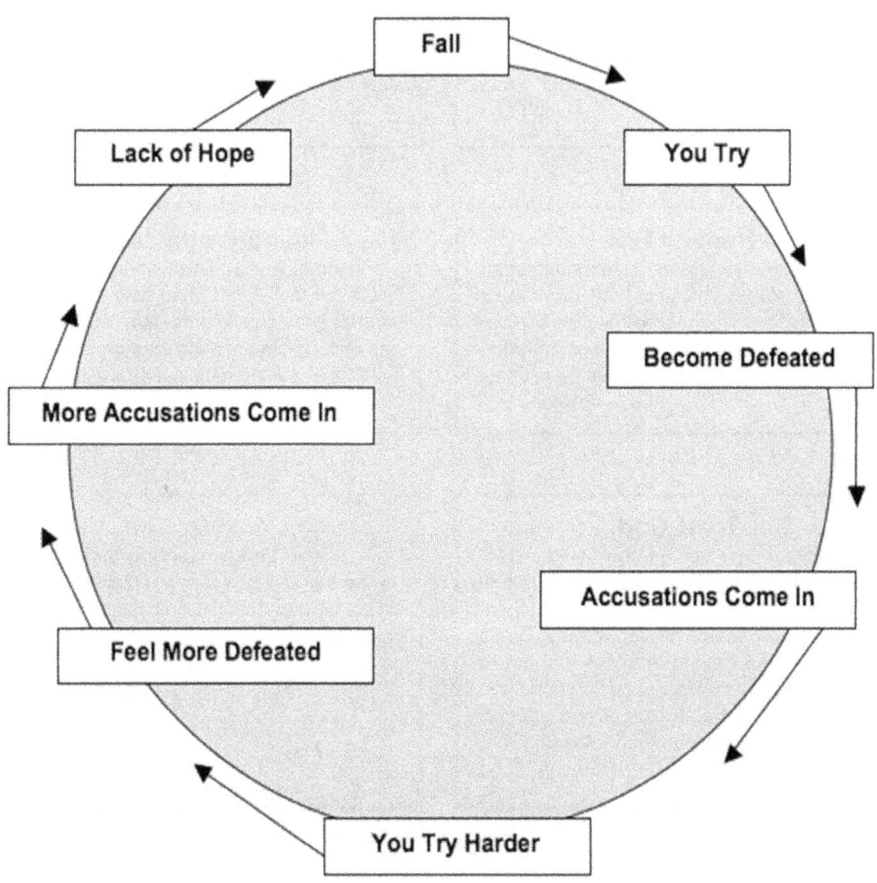

The Foundation Stones
Doctrine of Baptisms

THE GODLY CIRCLE OF EVENTS

Fall

Abide in God
"Remain in me, and I also remain in you. No branch can bear fruit by itself; it must remain in the vine. Neither can you bear fruit unless you remain in me. —John 15:4

You Repent From Sin
"If we confess our sins, he is faithful and just and will forgive us our sins and purify us from all unrighteousness."
—1 John 1:9

Hope in God
"For if, by the trespass of the one man, death reigned through that one man, how much more will those who receive God's abundant provision of grace and of the gift of righteousness reign in life through the one man, Jesus Christ." —Romans 5:17

Identify with Jesus
(Death, Burial, and Resurrection)
"We were therefore buried with him through baptism into death in order that, just as Christ was raised from the dead through the glory of the Father, we too may live a new life."
—Romans 6:4

Trust God
"Therefore, I urge you, brothers and sisters, in view of God's mercy, to offer your bodies as a living sacrifice, holy and pleasing to God —this is your true and proper worship. Do not conform to the pattern of this world, but be transformed by the renewing of your mind. Then you will be able to test and approve what God's will is—his good, pleasing, and perfect will." —Romans 12:1-2

Yield to God
(No Longer Serving Sin)
"In the same way, count yourselves dead to sin but alive to God in Christ Jesus. Therefore do not let sin reign in your mortal body so that you obey its evil desires."
—Romans 6:11-12

BAPTISM INTO THE HOLY SPIRIT

"He will baptize you with the Holy Spirit" —Matthew 3:11

In the first baptism *(the Baptism into Repentance)*, we talked about identifying with the holiness of **God the Father**. The *Baptism into Water* then led us to identification with the death, burial, and resurrection of **God the Son**. And that brings us to the *Baptism into the Holy Spirit* or **God the Holy Spirit** (the third Person of the Trinity). And the order of these baptisms is not accidental. The Holy Spirit is actually responsible for bringing us through this process of identification. By the Spirit, we are first drawn **to God** in repentance (through conviction), leading to Salvation. We are then led into a relationship **with Jesus** as we identify with the work of the Cross. Only then does the Holy Spirit reveal Himself to us in order that we might identify with Him.

Jesus' fulfillment of age-old messianic prophecies in the Old Testament has been greatly emphasized in Christian churches, and rightly so. But do you realize that the coming of the Holy Spirit was also foretold by many of the same prophets? Take a look at some examples below:

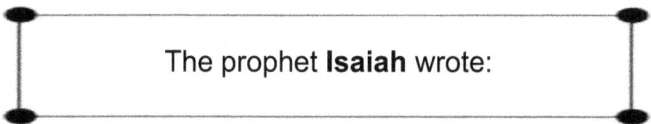

The prophet **Isaiah** wrote:

*"The fortress will be abandoned ... till **the Spirit is poured upon us from on high**, and the desert becomes a fertile field, and the fertile field seems like a forest."*
—Isaiah 32:15 (emphasis added)

The Foundation Stones
Doctrine of Baptisms

> God spoke through the prophet **Ezekiel**:

*"For I will take you out of the nations; I will gather you from all the countries and bring you back into your own land. I will sprinkle clean water on you, and you will be clean; I will cleanse you from all your impurities and from all your idols. I will give you a new heart and **put a new spirit in you**; I will remove from you your heart of stone and give you a heart of flesh. **And I will put my Spirit in you** and move you to follow my decrees and be careful to keep my laws."*
—Ezekiel 36:24-27 (emphasis added)

> God spoke through the prophet **Joel**:

*"And afterward, **I will pour out my Spirit on all people.** Your sons and daughters will prophesy, your old men will dream dreams, your young men will see visions. Even on my servants, both men and women, **I will pour out my Spirit in those days.**"*
—Joel 2:28-29 (emphasis added)

> **John the Baptist** spoke these words:

*"I baptize you with water for repentance. But after me comes one who is more powerful than I, whose sandals I am not worthy to carry. **He will baptize you with the Holy Spirit** and fire."*
—Matthew 3:11 (emphasis added)

The Foundation Stones
Doctrine of Baptisms

> These words were spoken by **Jesus** Himself:

> *"And I will ask the Father, and he will give you another **advocate** to help you and be with you forever—**the Spirit of truth**. The world cannot accept him, because it neither sees him nor knows him. But you know him, for he lives with you and will be in you."*
> —John 14:16-17 (emphasis added)

For all that the Bible says about the Holy Spirit, many churches today are surprisingly silent on the topic. In fact, most denominations have boiled the work of the Holy Spirit down to the highly-controversial manifestations that are attributed to the Spirit and then accept or reject His existence on this basis. In so doing, we have overlooked the Person of the Holy Spirit entirely, and we have missed out on the true purposes of His coming. The Holy Spirit is neither an emotion nor a magical spell. He is the Third Person of the Trinity, and He plays a critical role in the salvation and sanctification of believers. As a matter of fact, the Holy Spirit indwelling us is our connection to the heart of Heaven.

> *" 'For my thoughts are not your thoughts, neither are your ways my ways,' declares the Lord. 'As the heavens are higher than the earth, so are my ways higher than your ways and my thoughts than your thoughts.' "* —Isaiah 55:8-9

In a day and age where the scientific method and intellectual reasoning are set up as ideal, we struggle to identify with a God Who eludes our comprehension. We as a society chase after the illusion of CONTROL as if it were our life, and we likewise try to fit God into a structure that we can understand. But, just as the verse above tells us, God does not pretend to operate on our level. As a matter of fact, He tells us plainly that His ways are boyond us. And so we should not be surprised that the carnal mind disregards the things of God. We simply **cannot** receive or understand them apart from the revelation of the Holy Spirit.

The Foundation Stones
  Doctrine of Baptisms

In 1 Corinthians 2:14 we are told, *"The man without the Spirit does not accept the things that come from the Spirit of God but considers them foolishness, and cannot understand them because they are discerned only through the Spirit."*

> *"But as it is written:*
> *'Eye has not seen, nor ear heard,*
> *Nor have entered into the heart of man*
> *The things which God has prepared for those who love Him.'*
> ***But God has revealed them to us through His Spirit.*** *For the Spirit searches all things, yes, the deep things of God. For what man knows the things of a man except the spirit of the man which is in him? Even so no one knows the things of God except the Spirit of God.* ***Now we have received, not the spirit of the world, but the Spirit who is from God, that we might know the things that have been freely given to us by God.****"*
> 1 Corinthians 2:9-12 NKJV

Look at the privilege that we, the children of God, have been given. It is by the Holy Spirit alone that we can know and understand God's ways. As a matter of fact, the Holy Spirit is responsible for our very relationship with God and with Jesus. And what the world cannot understand has been supernaturally made known to us.

Let's take a minute to evaluate our level of intimacy with the Spirit of God. Write down anything that comes to mind when you think of the Holy Spirit:

_____   _____
_____   _____
_____   _____
_____   _____
_____   _____

We can expect to find in most lists such titles as Counselor, Comforter, Helper, Teacher, Person of the Trinity, and so on. But look at your list for a minute and see if you have named any PERSONALITY TRAITS among all of the titles. This may be a clue to how well you really **know** the Holy Spirit. Consider how you might identify a public figure by his roles in society (teacher, father, husband, etc). But, if that public figure were your father, you would instead describe him in terms of your intimate relationship with him. It is not so different with the Holy Spirit. We tend to imagine that He is a type of **entity** (a being, something that is not understood). But the truth is that the Holy Spirit is a **person**, and the Bible always presents Him this way. As a matter of fact, He is no less powerful, no less God than the rest of the Trinity. And, at the same time, He is our closest Companion and our greatest Advocate to Heaven's throne. The question is, have we identified with Him in this way? That is the essence of this baptism. Yes, the **power** of the Holy Spirit manifests in our walk with Him, but it must not be our priority. We must come to the Holy Spirit in order to **know Him** (*identification*). It is only through this relationship that we will recognize His work in and through us (*change*) and experience His power in our lives (*newness*).

> **IDENTIFICATION** with the Person of the Holy Spirit

> A **CHANGE** in perspective—to see the Holy Spirit

> The **NEWNESS** of power by walking in the Spirit

Let's identify some of the roles that the Holy Spirit plays in our lives:

The Holy Spirit produces God's fruit through us.

Galatians 5:22-23 (NKJV) tells us: *"But the **fruit of the Spirit** is love, joy, peace, longsuffering, kindness, goodness, faithfulness, gentleness, self-control"* (emphasis added*)*. These are actually some of the **personality traits** of the Holy Spirit. At the moment a person is born again, the Holy Spirit indwells and becomes one with the spirit of the person. And so the "personality" of the Holy Spirit (when we yield to Him) manifests in us. That is why we should be able to find evidence of God in any and every believer, not because we **imitate** holiness, but because the fullness of God is living within us!

The Holy Spirit reveals the things of God.

As we said earlier in the lesson, the Spirit's primary function is to reveal truth to us. First Corinthians 2:9-14 tells us that we cannot fathom the things of God but *"these are the things God has **revealed** to us by his Spirit"* (emphasis added). The scheme of the enemy is to keep us from knowing the Holy Spirit and so to be cut off from the revelation of the truth. The Holy Spirit is our Guide and Counselor. If we as Christians abandon His direction, we are left to forge our way through life disillusioned and oblivious to the things of God.

The Holy Spirit is our Comforter and Teacher.

John 14:26 (KJV) records Jesus' promise to the disciples that *"the **Comforter**, which is the Holy Ghost, whom the Father will send in my name, he shall **teach** you all things, and bring all things to your remembrance, whatsoever I have said unto you."* And so the role of the Holy Spirit in this verse is twofold. He not only comforts us with the truth, but He also instructs us in it. The Holy Spirit speaks to us in a still, small voice for sure. But He also speaks in a way that we can understand on an individual level. Do not be fooled. God KNOWS how to speak to you and me. The problem is that we have not learned to listen and be taught. The Spirit of God is the only part of the Trinity on the earth today. He is our spiritual Lifeline and the Keeper of our hearts.

The Holy Spirit is our Witness and Helper.

The Holy Spirit is given the role of assuring us not only of the truth but also of our salvation and our identity in Christ. In Romans 8:16 we are told that *"The Spirit himself **testifies** with our spirit that we are God's children"* (emphasis added). Several verses later we find that the Spirit (our Helper) also stands in the gap for us as we pray:

> *"In the same way, the Spirit **helps** us in our weakness. We do not know what we ought to pray for, but the Spirit himself intercedes for us through wordless groans. And he who searches our hearts knows the mind of the Spirit, because the Spirit intercedes for God's people in accordance with the will of God."*
> —Romans 8:26-27 (emphasis added)

The Holy Spirit is our Liberty and Life.

Second Corinthians 3:6 tells us that *"the letter kills, but the Spirit gives **life**."* And verse 17 of the same chapter adds, *"[W]here the Spirit of the Lord is, there is **freedom**"* (emphasis added). In these two statements we find a measure for our own lives. If we are walking in the Baptism of the Holy Spirit, the evidence will be freedom and life within us. Conversely, any area in which we are not experiencing these things is certainly not being empowered by the Spirit.

The Holy Spirit is our Anointing.

The book of Acts foretells the "pouring out of" the Spirit in anointing on believers. It says, *"In the last days, God says, I will pour out my Spirit on all people. Your sons and daughters will prophesy, your young men will see visions, your old men will dream dreams. Even on my servants, both men and women, I will pour out my Spirit in those days, and they will prophesy"* (Acts 2:17-18). The New Testament Church was the first to witness the anointing of the Holy Spirit, but we are recipients even today.

The Holy Spirit is our Power, Assurance, and Joy.

*"For our gospel did not come to you in word only, but also in **power**, and in the **Holy Spirit**, and in much **assurance** ... And you became followers of us and of the Lord, having received the word in much affliction, with **joy** of the Holy Spirit."* —1 Thessalonians 1:5-6 (NKJV) (emphasis added)

The Foundation Stones
   Doctrine of Baptisms

The power that is spoken of in the verse above is simply the power to live the Christian life. Most Christians are convinced that they have been commissioned by God to imitate or "act like" Jesus. And, while it may come across as a noble endeavor, it is actually an affront to the God who desires to simply live the life of Jesus THROUGH US. We **cannot** live the life of holiness and righteousness that we strive for. It is **only** the power of the Holy Spirit within you and me that accomplishes the things of God. We are just the vessels, void of life except for the life of God flowing through us. And it is here that assurance and joy is ours.

The Holy Spirit is our Fullness.

When we speak of being "filled by" the Holy Spirit, we are once again referring to a lifestyle and not any particular experience. Ephesians 4 warns us to be careful about how we live. We are called to be **filled** with the Spirit, so as to leave no room for the world in us. A good example would be the Corinthian church of Paul's time. In 1 Corinthians 3, Paul corrects a very Pentecostal and "Spirit-filled" church for their worldliness. God's concern is not that we experience manifestations of the Spirit but that we become intimately acquainted with the character of the Holy Spirit Himself.

Our first step in this baptism is to recognize the presence of the Holy Spirit within us on a daily basis. The Holy Spirit is first and foremost a PERSON. He was sent from God and IS God. But He is also the nearest of friends to whom we can tell our worst pains and fears without rejection. Simply ask Him to reveal Himself to you today, and then listen!

NOTES:

The Foundation Stones
Doctrine of Baptisms

BAPTISM INTO FIRE

"He will baptize you with the Holy Spirit and with fire"
—Matthew 3:11-12

The next baptism we are going to cover is the Baptism into Fire, which deals with the process of sanctification through the trials of God's fire. While this may not be the most appealing of the baptisms, it is nevertheless very real and critical to our walk with Him. Through the Baptism into Fire we are brought near to the heart of God and transformed into His likeness. We begin, once again, with the aspect of God's character that we are called to identify with—His PURITY.

IDENTIFICATION with the Purity of God

In Isaiah 6:5-7, the prophet recorded a vision that he experienced as part of his prophetic calling. Upon coming into the Presence of God, Isaiah was overwhelmed by his own sinfulness and the impurity of his heart. He spoke these words:

> *"Woe to me! ... I am ruined! For I am a man of unclean lips, and I live among a people of unclean lips, and my eyes have seen the King, the Lord Almighty"* (v. 5).

The Bible tells us that an angel of God then touched a fiery coal to Isaiah's lips and announced that his sin had been atoned for and his guilt taken away.

God desires to do the same with each of us. We must first be ushered into identification with God's purity and experience brokenness over the condition of our hearts before we will desire the fire of God. Possibly the best example in the Scriptures of a heart that was willing for God's fire is King David. Upon being exposed for his great sin before the people, David penned Psalm 51. It was a heartfelt plea to God that he might be cleansed from sin. David knew the journey of this baptism well, and he embraced it. In another psalm he also wrote these words:

The Foundation Stones
Doctrine of Baptisms

> *"Search me, God, and know my heart; test me and know my anxious thoughts. See if there is any offensive way in me, and lead me in the way everlasting."* —Psalm 139:23-24

It is up to you and me how far we want to go into the depths of His love and deliverance. And we must at this point choose if we are willing to walk through the fire of God—a process that will bring us into trials of many kinds—in order to experience all that He has for us. The verse below makes it clear that God is simply waiting for us to "open the door" to Him.

> *"I counsel you to buy from me gold refined in the fire, so you can become rich; and white clothes to wear, so you can cover your shameful nakedness; and salve to put on your eyes, so you can see. Those whom I love I rebuke and discipline. So be earnest, and repent. Here I am! I stand at the door and knock. If anyone hears my voice and opens the door, I will come in and eat with that person, and they with me."*
> —Revelation 3:18-20

If you find yourself wondering how God could desire that we go through the fire, be assured that you are not alone. Most of us cannot see beyond our pain to even consider the grander plan of God. Nor can we fathom a heavenly Father's cruelty in allowing His children to experience such trials. But the fact is that God not only ALLOWS us to walk through His fire, He **BECKONS** us to. And so we are left to trust that He has a purpose for it.

Let's consider the practical uses of fire in our day-to-day lives. Fire is used for two primary reasons. On one hand, it is able to BURN UP anything that is unwanted. And we could say the same is true of the fire of God. The Bible alludes to the destruction of this world by fire in the last days. We are told that everything that is not of God, as well as all unbelievers, will be consumed by His fire.

> *"[W]hen the Lord Jesus is revealed from heaven with His mighty angels, in flaming **fire** taking vengeance on those who do not know God,*

> *The Foundation Stones*
> *Doctrine of Baptisms*

and on those who do not obey the gospel of our Lord Jesus Christ."
—2 Thessalonians 1:7-8 (NKJV) (emphasis added)

*"By the same word the present heavens and earth are reserved for **fire**, being kept for the day of judgment and destruction of the ungodly."*
—2 Peter 3:7 (emphasis added)

*"But the day of the Lord will come like a thief. The heavens will disappear with a roar; the elements will be destroyed by **fire**, and the earth and everything done in it will be laid bare."*
—2 Peter 3:10 (emphasis added)

The second purpose for fire is to PURIFY what **is** of value. Precious metals, for instance, are never destroyed by fire. Rather, they are purified by it, and the end result is a more valuable piece of material. This is the aspect of God's fire that is dealt with in this baptism. Within you and me, the fire of God "burns up" anything that is not of Him. And through this process we are **purified** as gold.

> **CHANGE** brought about as God removes the dross

- **Dross** – Impurity or debris mixed in with the pure.[4]

We love God and seek to know Him deeper, but it is the dross in our lives that distorts our view of His love. We have prayed, "I want to know you more," and so He brings us through the Baptism into Fire so that we may. When we place ourselves in God's hands, He will surely remove anything and everything in us that does not produce life. Oftentimes, these are the very things that men esteem (pride, independence, etc.) that hinder our walk with God.

The Foundation Stones
  Doctrine of Baptisms

In John 15:2, Jesus told his disciples, *"He cuts off every branch in me that bears no fruit, while every branch that does bear fruit he prunes so that it will be even more fruitful."*

> *"I baptize you with water for repentance. But after me comes one who is more powerful than I, whose sandals I am not fit to carry. He will baptize you with the Holy Spirit and fire. His winnowing fork is in his hand, and he will clear his threshing floor, gathering his wheat into the barn and burning up the chaff with unquenchable fire."*
> —Matthew 3:11-12

Notice in John the Baptist's description of the Baptism into Fire that God is gathering **HIS** wheat before burning up the chaff. That is to say that the only things that are of any value to Him are HIS things. Nothing of the world and nothing that is generated by the efforts of the flesh (even "good" things) will withstand the fire of God. What God wants in you and me is only what has been put there by Him! We can rest assured that we will not be destroyed by His fire (as will the things of the world), but we can also count on walking away from it with less of **ourselves**.

> *"For no one can lay any foundation other than the one already laid, which is Jesus Christ. If anyone builds on this foundation using gold, silver, costly stones, wood, hay or straw, their work will be shown for what it is, because the Day will bring it to light. It will be revealed with fire, and the fire will test the quality of each person's work. If what has been built survives, the builder will receive a reward. If it is burned up, the builder will suffer loss but yet will be saved—even though only as one escaping through the flames."*
> —1 Corinthians 3:11-15

The verse above makes it clear that our "buildings" (that which we compose our lives of) will be shown for what they are. And the loss we will suffer is the fruitfulness of God in our lives. First Peter 4 talks about suffering for God's glory. He makes a clear distinction between the suffering that results

The Foundation Stones
Doctrine of Baptisms

from being a Christian (that which Christ endured) and the suffering that comes from taking part in the ways of the world. We, the Body of Christ, are called to correction and discipline NOW so that we may escape the judgment that is to come upon the world.

> *"For it is time for judgment to begin with God's household; and if it begins with us, what will the outcome be for those who do not obey the gospel of God? And, 'If it is hard for the righteous to be saved, what will become of the ungodly and the sinner?'"*
> —1 Peter 4:17-18

You see, we must not only allow God to put us through the fire; we must also walk in the reality of His purifying work. We cannot step into the hands of God until we choose to separate ourselves from the world, and this is the point at which many of us find ourselves. Look at the Scriptures below and consider the call that God has placed on your life.

> *"Nevertheless, God's solid foundation stands firm, sealed with this inscription: 'The Lord knows those who are his,' and, 'Everyone who confesses the name of the Lord must turn away from wickedness.' In a large house there are articles not only of gold and silver, but also of wood and clay; some are for special purposes and some for common use. Those who cleanse themselves from the latter will be instruments for special purposes, made holy, useful to the Master and prepared to do any good work."* —2 Timothy 2:19-21

> *"Do not be yoked together with unbelievers. For what do righteousness and wickedness have in common? Or what fellowship can light have with darkness? What harmony is there between Christ and Belial? Or what does a believer have in common with an unbeliever? What agreement is there between the temple of God and idols? For we are the temple of the living God. As God has said: 'I will live with them and walk among them, and I will be their God, and they will be my people.' Therefore, 'Come out from them and be separate, says the*

> *Lord. Touch no unclean thing, and I will receive you.' And, 'I will be a Father to you, and you will be my sons and daughters, says the Lord Almighty.'"* —2 Corinthians 6:14-18

NEWNESS of being drawn into His likeness

The newness that results from identification with the purity of God is that we are drawn into His likeness. Through the Baptism into Fire, Christ purifies the church *"to make her holy, cleansing her by the washing with water through the word, and to present her to himself as a radiant church, without stain or wrinkle or any other blemish, but holy and blameless"* (Ephesians 5:26-27).

Below are some verses to hold to concerning this baptism. They point us to the powerful purposes and plans of God that are worked out through much pain and testing. We must always keep our eyes on Him when we walk through the fire, for He promises that He will be with us in the midst of it (Isaiah 43:1-2).

> *"For you, God, tested us; you refined us like silver. You brought us into prison and laid burdens on our backs. You let people ride over our heads; we went through fire and water, but you brought us to a place of abundance."* —Psalm 66:10-12

> *"In all this you greatly rejoice, though now for a little while you may have had to suffer grief in all kinds of trials. These have come so that the proven genuineness of your faith—of greater worth than gold, which perishes even though refined by fire—may result in praise, glory and honor when Jesus Christ is revealed."* —1 Peter 1:6-8

> *"But he knows the way that I take; when he has tested me, I will come forth as gold."* —Job 23:10

BAPTISM INTO HIS BODY

"For we were all baptized by one spirit into one body"
—1 Corinthians 12:13

When we speak about the body of Christ, which is the focal point of this baptism, it is always best to start with the principal of marriage. After all, the Scriptures speak about Christ and His body in terms of the relationship between a husband and wife. And so we might say that marriage as God has meant it to be is the earthly picture of Christ and His **BRIDE** (the body of believers).

> *"As a young man marries a young woman, so will your Builder marry you; as a bridegroom rejoices over his bride, so will your God rejoice over you."* —Isaiah 62:5

God views marriage as the coming together of two persons to form one body. In Genesis 2:24, the term *"one flesh"* was used to describe the first marriage union, that of Adam and Eve. When the Pharisees questioned Jesus about divorce (see Matthew 19:3-6), Jesus reminded them that a man and his wife *"are no longer two, but one flesh. Therefore what God has joined together, let no one separate."* The oneness of the body in marriage can be viewed as the loss of individual identity comparable to mixing together two portions of water to create one. And this points us to the reality of spiritual oneness in Christ. Just as God is supernaturally able to make two people one in marriage, we who are born again have become one with God in spirit, never to be separated.

> *"Do you not know that your bodies are members of Christ himself? Shall I then take the members of Christ and unite them with a prostitute? Never! Do you not know that he who unites himself with a prostitute is one with her in body? For it is said, 'The two will become one flesh.' But whoever is united with the Lord is one with him in spirit."* —1 Corinthians 6:15-17

The Foundation Stones
  Doctrine of Baptisms

The verse below has been widely criticized in recent years because it upholds the value of submission in the marriage relationship, an ideal that has long since been dismissed as degrading and old-fashioned. But the essence of this verse forms the backbone of the Baptism into His Body, and so we might do well to reconsider its relevance to our lives. In it we find glimpses into the relationship between Christ and the church, His body. The body of Christ is called to submit to Christ as a wife to her husband. There is certainly no way around this point. But notice that the emphasis is placed on the duty of the husband, that he must lay down his life out of love for his wife, just as Christ has done for the church. It is actually quite ironic that this powerful call to sacrificial love and honor has become the target of accusations of sexism in today's world.

> *"Wives, submit yourselves to your own husbands as you do to the Lord. For the husband is the head of the wife as Christ is the head of the church,* **his body***, of which he is the Savior. Now as the church submits to Christ, so also wives should submit to their husbands in everything. Husbands, love your wives, just as Christ loved the church and gave himself up for her to make her holy, cleansing her by the washing with water through the word, and to present her to himself as a radiant church, without stain or wrinkle or any other blemish, but holy and blameless. In this same way, husbands ought to love their wives as their own bodies. He who loves his wife loves himself. After all, no one ever hated their own body, but they feed and care for their body, just as Christ does the church—for we are members of* **his body***. 'For this reason a man will leave his father and mother and be united to his wife, and the two will become one flesh.' This is a profound mystery—but I am talking about Christ and the church."*
>   —Ephesians 5:22-32 (emphasis added)

It is no wonder that our role as the body of Christ is so hard for us to understand and accept. If we take a look at the institution of marriage in today's world, we will see that we have missed the heart of it altogether. There is little to be found along the lines of commitment between man and wife. Why do we expect the body of Christ to have fared any better? Because we have not understood the love of Christ for us, we have not identified ourselves fully with Him and His purposes. Neither has the body of Christ as a whole united as we have been called to do.

> *"Just as a body, though one, has many parts, but all its many parts form one body, so it is with Christ. For we were all baptized by one Spirit so as to form one body—whether Jews or Gentiles, slave or free—and we were all given the one Spirit to drink. Even so the body is not made up of one part but of many. Now if the foot should say, 'Because I am not a hand, I do not belong to the body,' it would not for that reason stop being part of the body. And if the ear should say, 'Because I am not an eye, I do not belong to the body,' it would not for that reason stop being part of the body. If the whole body were an eye, where would the sense of hearing be? If the whole body were an ear, where would the sense of smell be? But in fact God has placed the parts in the body, every one of them, just as he wanted them to be. If they were all one part, where would the body be? As it is, there are many parts, but one body. The eye cannot say to the hand, 'I don't need you!' And the head cannot say to the feet, 'I don't need you!' On the contrary, those parts of the body that seem to be weaker are indispensable, and the parts that we think are less honorable we treat with special honor. And the parts that are unpresentable are treated with special modesty, while our presentable parts need no special treatment. But God has put the body together, giving greater honor to the parts that lacked it, so that there should be no division in the body, but that its parts should have equal concern for each other. If one part suffers, every part suffers with it; if one part is honored, every part rejoices with it. Now you are the body of Christ, and each one of you is a part of it."* —1 Corinthians 12:12-27

The Baptism into His Body begins with our identification with both the universal body of Christ and the local body of Christ. The former comes with the experience of being born again, for we as Christians have all been made a part of His body. The latter is experienced by choice. It is only through the local church that we can take part in the functioning body of Christ on this earth.

> **IDENTIFICATION** with His local and universal body

There are so many "options" in the way of churches today that it seems unnecessary and maybe even unwise to commit to any one. And the sad consequence of this is that most of us never commit at all. Were we left to our own devices, we might never seek out relationships with another—even in marriage. After all, the human nature is selfish above all things. But God placed within us a desire and a need to live "outside of" ourselves and to be connected with others. The biggest hurdle in this baptism, then, is the independent mindset that has been taught and encouraged in us. We strive continually to be self-sufficient only to find out that God did not design us to be. In Romans 14:7, for example, we are told that *"none of us lives to himself alone and none of us dies to himself alone."*

It is only through reaching out and committing ourselves to others that we as humans find fulfillment. And we have seen some very startling proofs of this in unexpected places. Take, for instance, the Japanese soldiers of World War II. They were so dedicated to their emperor that they **willingly** laid down their lives to the point of death. And for this reason, they were a very formidable and almost unconquerable foe. We also see this in cultic organizations as well as gangs, where members forfeit their lives in commitment to the others in the group and to the purposes of the organization. These groups are so popular and powerful simply because they offer **identity** and **unity**. And in this sense, they are actually mimicking the body of Christ, as it ought to be.

God has actually created us to be dependent on Him and also on others in the body of Christ. After all, parts of a physical body certainly cannot function independently of one another. A body is only a body because it operates in unison. And so it is with us. If we have counted fellowship with other believers as unnecessary, then we have been deceived, and we need to align ourselves with His purposes.

> A **CHANGE** in perspective—no longer seeing ourselves as separate from others

In Romans 8:35-39 we are assured that, in reality, nothing *"will be able to separate us from the love of God that is in Christ Jesus our Lord."* But in experience we have to admit that we feel far from His presence and His power sometimes. The enemy wants nothing more than for us to see ourselves as separated from God and from His church so that we might never experience Christ in one another.

> *"And let us consider how we may spur one another on toward love and good deeds, not giving up meeting together, as some are in the habit of doing, but let us encourage one another."*
> —Hebrews 10:24-25

In the book of Romans, Paul encouraged the believers to recognize their place in the body of Christ. In Romans 12:4-5 we read, *"For just as each of us has one body with many members, and these members do not all have the same function, so in Christ we, though many, form one body, and each member belongs to all the others."* We will never function as a body until we realize that we cannot function independently. We are so used to "church organization" and social gathering that most of us have never even been exposed to a functioning body. And, as a matter of fact, this is the very thing that the enemy resists the most because with the body of Christ comes power and anointing.

> The **NEWNESS** of functioning as one whole body

Ask yourself whether or not you are willing to lose your identity to take your place in the body of Christ. Are we seeking God for understanding of our connections with others? The body of Christ is not an organization of

The Foundation Stones
Doctrine of Baptisms

believers but a COMMUNITY of believers, and God is able to supernaturally connect us as He does in marriage so that we may function as one. The divisions that we see in churches today are a result of our independent visions. God is calling His own to take up the vision of the body of Christ.

NOTES:

The Functioning Body of Christ

The most prevalent obstacle to the functioning body of Christ, as we have already identified, is our independence of and separation from other believers. In this case we might say that we are avoiding our participation in the church body as God intended. But there are also those who simply misunderstand its purpose and function. We can earnestly pursue connections with other believers but end up with codependent relationships if we fail to depend solely on Christ, who is the "Head," to lead us. Even those in leadership can make the mistake of trying to meet the needs within the congregation and, in doing so, rob them of the experience of God's provision.

Because there is so much deception in our churches regarding this issue, it is critical that we line up our beliefs with the Word of God. The Bible identifies several primary functions of the local body of Christ:

1. **Teaching**
2. **Confirmation**
3. **Worship**
4. **Ministry**
5. **Fellowship**

But the purposes of a united body go far beyond Sunday services. Those who determine to take their places in the body of Christ must be aware of the enemy's schemes if they are to stand firm. Many times in the Scriptures, Jesus speaks of the church body in terms of a flock of sheep, and in so doing He makes several analogies that are important for us to understand.

> "I am the good shepherd. The good shepherd lays down his life for the sheep. The hired hand is not the shepherd and does not own the sheep. So when he sees the wolf coming, he abandons the sheep and runs away. Then the wolf attacks the flock and scatters it. The man runs away because he is a hired hand and cares nothing for the sheep."
> —John 10:11-13

The Foundation Stones
  Doctrine of Baptisms

First of all, notice what the wolf accomplishes by attacking the sheep. We are told that he causes them to **scatter**, which is their natural reaction when frightened. It is a very effective strategy considering that the only natural defense sheep have is huddling together. Can you see the parallel? The body of Christ can only exist when the members remain united. Our sole protection as a body is our connection with one another. And, consequently, we see our spiritual enemy working diligently in the local church to scatter the members. He knows that we have no chance when we are isolated and without covering.

The tricky thing about the enemy's attacks on the body of Christ is that they often come from within in the form of offense, backbiting, strife, etc., between the members. And so, more often than not, we fail to recognize the hand of the enemy at work, and we, instead, take up our cases against one another. In Acts 20, Paul warns the Ephesian church about this very thing.

> *"I know that after I leave, savage wolves will come in among you and will not spare the flock. Even from your own number men will arise and distort the truth in order to draw away disciples after them. So be on your guard!"* —Acts 20:29-31

Jesus, who called Himself the "good shepherd," laid out an immovable standard by which all of the workings within the body can be measured. In Luke 11:23, He said, *"Whoever is not with me is against me, and whoever does not **gather** with me **scatters**"* (emphasis added). You see, in God's eyes, there is no middle ground. Anything that divides rather than uniting believers is positively not of God. And so our responsibility in the body of Christ is two-fold. We must not only perceive the schemes of the enemy at work and stand united, but we must also guard our own hearts and minds in order that we might not open ourselves up to be used as his instruments of division.

Some of the sternest judgments of God recorded in the Bible are aimed at the "shepherds of Israel" who were assigned to guard and lead God's flock.

They were charged with scattering and neglecting those for whom they were to lay down their lives. We already saw in John 10 that the "hired hand" quickly deserted the flock in a time of danger. But there are sadly those who would manipulate the body of Christ for personal gain alone. Look at the following verses, for example:

"Woe to the shepherds who are destroying and scattering the sheep of my pasture! ... Because you have scattered my flock and driven them away and have not bestowed care on them, I will bestow punishment on you for the evil you have done." —Jeremiah 23:1-2

"This is what the Sovereign Lord says: Woe to the shepherds of Israel who only take care of themselves! Should not shepherds take care of the flock? You eat the curds, clothe yourselves with the wool and slaughter the choice animals, but you do not take care of the flock. You have not strengthened the weak or healed the sick or bound up the injured. You have not brought back the strays or searched for the lost. You have ruled them harshly and brutally. So they were scattered because there was no shepherd, and when they were scattered they became food for all the wild animals. My sheep wandered over all the mountains and on every high hill. They were scattered over the whole earth, and no one searched or looked for them."
—Ezekiel 34:2-6

The true shepherd's heart is easily recognized by its passion to **serve** and **gather**. And the same can be said for the sheep. But it is only by revelation of the Holy Spirit that we can see the fullness of the body of Christ. We find in Ezekiel 37:1-2 a powerful vision that concerns the body of Christ. In this account we are told that Ezekiel was brought to a valley full of dry bones and asked the question, *"Son of man, can these bones live?"* The Lord was preparing Ezekiel to perceive spiritually what was yet to be seen in the physical. And Ezekiel's response was this: *"Sovereign Lord, you alone know."*

What Ezekiel was about to witness was the hand of God miraculously

The Foundation Stones
Doctrine of Baptisms

connecting together the bones and breathing life into the bodies. And in a matter of moments, a vast army stood before him. It is a picture of the body of Christ, a body that appears to be lifeless and beyond repair in our eyes. But God has committed to connect and draw His body together. The power of the body is in its connections, and it is here that life begins to flow. As God breathes His life into us, we will rise up as a united front in His strength. If you cannot quite imagine it, ask God to reveal it to you as He did for Ezekiel. But, most importantly, we need to believe that what God has decreed will come to pass. Our responsibility is to be connected with others so that we might take our place in the battle. It is not an option for us. It is where we belong.

> *"From him the whole body, joined and held together by every supporting ligament, grows and builds itself up in love, as each part does its work."* —Ephesians 4:16

NOTES:

BAPTISM INTO SUFFERING

"You will drink the cup I drink and be baptized with the baptism I am baptized with." —Mark 10:39

How does one justify the idea that a loving God would allow and even initiate suffering in the lives of His children? It is a difficult concept to grasp and so, quite often, the subject is avoided altogether in churches. But it is a reality that we cannot get around. Not only does God allow righteous men to suffer for no apparent reason, He actually orchestrated the worst and most humiliating of deaths for His only begotten Son. Isaiah 53:10 (NKJV) even goes so far as to say, *"Yet it **pleased** the Lord to bruise Him; He has put Him to grief"* (emphasis added). And so we must come to terms with the fact that suffering somehow plays a part in the grand scheme of things and that His perfect will includes OUR suffering as well.

Can you imagine a parent arranging their child's circumstances with the purpose of causing pain and heartache? We cringe at the thought, for such an act would be considered malicious on human terms. And so we also struggle to make sense of the suffering all around us over which we **know** our God is sovereign. Consequently, this baptism is a very important one for us to understand. We cannot afford to turn our backs on the realities of this life any more than we can afford to misinterpret God's heart toward us. Oswald Chambers had this to say in his book, "My Utmost for His Highest":

> **"Unless we can look the darkest, blackest fact full in the face without damaging God's character, we do not yet know Him."**[1]

It is easy to thank God for His many blessings, but how many Christians are sure enough of God's heart for them that they are able to thank Him in times of suffering as well? It is only in suffering that we really get to KNOW God and understand that His grace is sufficient for us (see 2 Corinthians 12:10). If we find ourselves doubting His character when trouble arises, we can be sure that we have been **keeping ourselves** from this very thing.

The Foundation Stones
   Doctrine of Baptisms

The Baptism into Fire, as you may recall, also deals with God's allowance of trials and pain in our lives. But the Baptism into Suffering is very different in its **purpose**. While the trial by fire is intended for our **own** purification and sanctification, the Baptism into Suffering is primarily for OTHERS.

> *"But He was wounded for our transgressions, He was bruised for our iniquities; the chastisement for our peace was upon Him, and by His stripes we are healed."* —Isaiah 53:5 (NKJV)

Consider, for a moment, the suffering of Jesus. It was not for His own benefit but for **ours** that He endured what He did. Jesus' sacrifice of suffering was the supreme show of God's love for us. It was allowed so that we might be healed and delivered. Hebrews 2:10 (NKJV) tells us that Jesus was made *"perfect through sufferings."* The author of Hebrews goes on to say this:

> *"Son though he was, he learned obedience from what he suffered and, once made perfect, he became the source of eternal salvation for all who obey him"* —Hebrews 5:8-9

Are you wondering why Jesus, who was already without sin, had to be made perfect through suffering? What these verses are alluding to is the perfect demonstration of the love of God that comes only through suffering. Jesus' sacrifice made God's love complete. Likewise, the perfect manifestation of God's love to the world today is accomplished through you and me as we walk through this baptism. **God chooses to bring suffering into our lives in order that we might reveal Jesus to a lost world.**

IDENTIFICATION with His suffering

Suffering brings about brokenness, which serves one main purpose in God's economy. We are broken so that God's life might freely flow through us to others. We are like the earthen vessel spoken of in Mark 14:3. We must be broken to reveal the treasure within, which is Jesus Christ. And that is why the Bible places such a high premium on the broken and contrite heart (see Isaiah 57:15, as well as Psalm 51:17 and 34:18).

> *"These are the ones I look on with favor: those who are humble and contrite in spirit, and who tremble at my word."* —Isaiah 66:2

As is true with all of the baptisms, we will only enter the Baptism into Suffering by choice. Certainly, suffering is an unavoidable part of life. Those who are unsaved suffer for their sins, but we as the children of God have been given the privilege of suffering for His glory. We find an almost humorous account of two disciples, James and John, asking Jesus to grant them places of honor in heaven. And Jesus' reply was this:

> *"You don't know what you are asking. ... Can you drink the cup I drink or be baptized with the baptism I am baptized with?"*
> —Mark 10:35-40

Although the disciples did not understand this at the time, Jesus was speaking about the cup of God's will and the Baptism into Suffering. We, like the original disciples, must come to the point where our love for Jesus is more important than our own lives. And this is where God is able to entrust us with His "cups" of suffering.

We find later in the New Testament many examples of suffering as the disciples, motivated by their love for Christ, canvassed the known world with the Good News. Most of their persecution came from the "religious" groups that had treated Jesus likewise. None of these men pretended that their suffering was pleasant. Even Jesus, shortly before His arrest, pleaded: *"My Father, if it is possible, may this cup be taken from me. Yet not as I will, but as you will"* (Matthew 26:39). There is no getting around the pain of it. But notice in the verse on the next page the undertone of hope and purpose in Paul's words, for he knew that his suffering would bring peace to others.

The Foundation Stones
  Doctrine of Baptisms

> *"For it seems to me that God has put us apostles on display at the end of the procession, like men condemned to die in the arena. We have been made a spectacle to the whole universe, to angels as well as to human beings. We are fools for Christ, but you are so wise in Christ! We are weak, but you are strong! You are honored, we are dishonored! To this very hour we go hungry and thirsty, we are in rags, we are brutally treated, we are homeless. We work hard with our own hands. When we are cursed, we bless; when we are persecuted, we endure it; when we are slandered, we answer kindly. We have become the scum of the earth, the garbage of the world—right up to this moment."*
> —1 Corinthians 4:9-13

Sadly enough, many churches today do not so much as approach the subject of suffering for Christ's sake. The body of Christ has been lulled to sleep by feel-good messages and prosperity doctrines. And we do everything we can to avoid suffering, however noble the cause. But there really is no way around persecution and suffering if we intend to live righteously. In 2 Timothy 3:12 Paul says, *"[E]veryone who wants to live a godly life in Christ Jesus will be persecuted."* Jesus warned us time and again that the world would hate us because of him (see Matthew 10:22). In fact, we are told that we will be persecuted by those who believe they are *"offering a service to God"* by doing so (see John 16:2-3).

> *"Remember what I told you: 'A servant is not greater than his master.' If they persecuted me, they will persecute you also."* —John 15:20

Furthermore, we stand to lose a great deal by avoiding this commission. Suffering for the name of Jesus is not something we have been called to endure but rather an honor that we have been granted. Jesus included this as a "BLESSING" in the Beatitudes (see Matthew 5:11-12). Alongside the meek, the merciful, and the poor in spirit, Jesus counted those who suffered persecution to be blessed by God. And, although Jesus' disciples stumbled over the concept at the time, they soon experienced this joy for themselves. In Acts 5:41 we are told that the apostles who had just been flogged for their

The Foundation Stones
Doctrine of Baptisms

beliefs *"left the Sanhedrin, rejoicing because they had been counted worthy of suffering disgrace for the Name."*

"For it has been granted to you on behalf of Christ not only to believe in him, but also to suffer for him." —Philippians 1:29

"Dear friends, do not be surprised at the fiery ordeal that has come on you to test you, as though something strange were happening to you. But rejoice inasmuch as you participate in the sufferings of Christ, so that you may be overjoyed when his glory is revealed. If you are insulted because of the name of Christ, you are blessed, for the Spirit of glory and of God rests on you. If you suffer, it should not be as a murderer or thief or any other kind of criminal, or even as a meddler. However, if you suffer as a Christian, do not be ashamed, but praise God that you bear that name ... So then, those who suffer according to God's will should commit themselves to their faithful Creator and continue to do good." —1 Peter 4:12-19

The Bible clearly distinguishes between suffering that is a result of our sin and suffering for our faith. When we step into this baptism, the change that takes place is the **loss of self**. First Peter 4:1-2 tells us that *"he who has suffered in his body is done with sin. ... He does not live the rest of his earthly life for evil human desires, but rather for the will of God."* To identify with the suffering of Christ is to die to sin's hold on our lives. And this is the place at which the only thing that matters to us is the will of God. How we have longed to be found with this resolve. And yet, how we have avoided the process. God will never circumvent our wills in this matter. Instead, He waits for us to willingly drink from His cup.

> A heart-**CHANGE** evidenced by the loss of self

To enter into this baptism is to willingly sacrifice ourselves for the sake of others and, in turn, to find our lives in Him.

The Foundation Stones
Doctrine of Baptisms

> *"Whoever finds their life will lose it, and whoever loses their life for my sake will find it."* —Matthew 10:39

We may bless others by the things we do or say, but suffering to reveal the love of God will change us and others for eternity. Consider it a gift from God, for He trusts you and me to show the world His love. And the result is the salvation of many people, those who are witnessing the sufficiency of God in the midst of our suffering. That is what the world needs to see.

The **NEWNESS** of many people born again

While the direct result of the Baptism into Suffering is the salvation of others, it also brings about the establishment and strengthening of those who walk through it. Through these experiences we become immovable in our faith.

> *"And the God of all grace, who called you to his eternal glory in Christ, after you have suffered a little while, will himself restore you and make you strong, firm, and steadfast."* —1 Peter 5:10

NOTES:

BAPTISM INTO THE CLOUD

> *"Our forefathers were all under the cloud ... They were all baptized into Moses in the cloud."* —1 Corinthians 10:1-2

The last and maybe the most unfamiliar baptism that we need to address is the Baptism into the Cloud. The very name conveys a type of mystery and uncertainty. However, you might be surprised to know that the concept finds its basis in one of the best-known Biblical accounts—the Great Exodus. And this is where we want to start our study.

We are told that during the great deliverance of the Israelites from bondage in Egypt, God dwelt among them in the form of a **cloud**. And this cloud came to represent several significant functions of God in their everyday lives.

In the Old Testament, the CLOUD represented:

I.
The *tangible presence* of God

> *"By day the Lord went ahead of them in a pillar of cloud to guide them on their way."* —Exodus 13:21

If we were to read through the Exodus account in its entirety, we would find that God went out of His way time and again to make His presence known to the Israelites (and to the Egyptians, for that matter). From the plagues to the parting of the Red Sea, God's power was demonstrated in grand proportions on behalf of His people. But He did not stop there. Shrouded in a cloud, God dwelt among the Israelites throughout their journey. And, in this way, His presence was made tangible and real to a fearful and easily disheartened people.

II.
The *protection* of God

When the Egyptians pursued the Israelites to the brink of the Red Sea, we are told that the pillar of cloud (and God Himself) moved behind the Israelites, creating a barrier between them and their enemies. The Israelites, although they were justifiably frightened, could have no doubt of God's determination to protect them from harm.

> *"Then the angel of God, who had been traveling in front of Israel's army, withdrew and went behind them. The pillar of cloud also moved from in front and stood behind them, coming between the armies of Egypt and Israel. Throughout the night the cloud brought darkness to the one side and light to the other side; so neither went near the other all night long."* —Exodus 14:19-20

III.
The *direction* and *timing* of God

We are also told that God Himself searched out the path ahead of the Israelites as they traveled. His presence was their guide, and they were dependent on His leading moment by moment.

> *"In spite of this, you did not trust in the Lord your God, who went ahead of you on your journey, in fire by night and in a cloud by day, to search out places for you to camp and show you the way you should go."*
> —Deuteronomy 1:32-33

IV.
Fellowship with and *worship* of God

The following Scripture conveys the idea that the cloud was a vehicle by which God and Moses were able to fellowship together while the people stood at a distance and worshiped. The Israelites as a whole responded to the presence of God with fear and apprehension. As 2 Chronicles 5:13-14 reminds us, the cloud itself enveloped "the glory of the Lord."

> *"As Moses went into the tent, the pillar of cloud would come down and stay at the entrance, while the Lord spoke with Moses. Whenever the people saw the pillar of cloud standing at the entrance to the tent, they all stood and worshiped, each at the entrance to their tent."*
> —Exodus 33:9-10

V.
The *Fresh Anointing* of God

Lastly, the cloud represented the fresh anointing of God. It is not as if God informed His people of their destination and then left them to forge their way through the wilderness. The Israelites waited on the moving of God's presence, and they dared not venture beyond it. Their eyes were ever fixed on the cloud for their present needs.

> *"In all the travels of the Israelites, whenever the cloud lifted from above the tabernacle, they would set out; but if the cloud did not lift, they did not set out—until the day it lifted."* —Exodus 40:36-37

Obviously, there is more to this baptism than the singular experience of the Israelites as they were led out of Egypt. Although it is a fascinating account, we would be hard-pressed to salvage a present-day application to our lives were it not for a parallel truth that is revealed in the New Testament. By way of prophecy, Isaiah points us to this reality that was still far off at the time. He says, in Isaiah 4:5-6, that *"the Lord will create over all of Mount Zion and over those who assemble there a cloud."* It was a prophecy that the cloud would rest upon His temple, which we now know is YOU and ME.

The role of the "cloud" in the Old Testament, which was to represent the presence, protection, and direction of God, has been given to the Holy Spirit who dwells within us.

The Foundation Stones
  Doctrine of Baptisms

In John 16:5-16, Jesus explained the work of the Holy Spirit to His disciples. He assured them that His death would open the door for the tangible presence of God to be sent to the earth in the person of the Holy Spirit. This time, however, the children of God would be directed and led not by an object in the sky but from within. And this is the essence of the Baptism into the Cloud. It is the identification with the leading of the Holy Spirit.

> **IDENTIFICATION** with the leading of the Spirit

God has promised the Spirit to all who are born again, just as the "cloud" of Moses' time was present for all who followed behind it. But we must choose to partake in this reality. First Corinthians 10:1-5 reminds us that, although *"our ancestors were all under the cloud"* and experienced the same provision, many of them failed to embrace the reality of God's presence by faith, and they consequently missed out on the Promised Land. When we identify ourselves with the leading of the Spirit and respond in obedience, the result will be the abandonment of our own plans and devices for the reality of moving with God's heart.

> **CHANGE** of guidance—away from my own planning

Let's address some basic questions that come up regarding this baptism and the concept of being led by the Spirit.

Can a person really be led by the Spirit?

The first practical example of being led by the indwelling Spirit is found in the New Testament account of Jesus' life. We are told, for example, that *"Jesus, being filled with the Holy Spirit, returned from the Jordan and was **led by the Spirit** into the wilderness"* (Luke 4:1 NKJV emphasis added). Every aspect of Jesus' life and ministry revolved around obedience to the direction of God given by the Holy Spirit.

Although we could find no better example of a Spirit-led individual, Jesus' experiences may not seem the most relevant to our day-to-day lives. So let's look a little farther into the New Testament at the first generation of Spirit-filled believers. The book of Acts tells us that the Holy Spirit actively communicated with the disciples in practical matters of direction and guidance. In Acts 13:2 the Spirit ordered the setting apart of Barnabas and Saul for His special calling. And in Acts 16:6, we are told that *"Paul and his companions traveled throughout the region of Phrygia and Galatia, **having been kept by the Holy Spirit** from preaching the word in the province of Asia"* (emphasis added).

NEWNESS of being led by the Spirit

The New Testament makes it plain to us that the Holy Spirit's purpose is always current and relevant to our lives. God speaks to us PRESENTLY through the Spirit, and we are called to simply move according to His leading. We are no longer under the "old way" of the law. Rather, the law of God has been written on our hearts by means of God's Spirit.

> *"He has made us competent as ministers of a new covenant—not of the letter but of the Spirit; for the letter kills, but the Spirit gives life."*
> —2 Corinthians 3:6

> *"[W]e have been released from the law so that we serve in the new way of the Spirit, and not in the old way of the written code."*
> —Romans 7:6

Is it important to be led by the Spirit?

The Bible tells us that being led by the Spirit is what identifies you and me as children of God. It should be the trademark of our faith and the one thing that sets us apart from the rest of the world. Romans 8:14 puts it this way:

> *"For those who are led by the Spirit of God are the children of God."*

Furthermore, we are called to live by the Spirit so that we might not be controlled by the sinful nature. If we fail to respond to the direction of the Holy Spirit in our day-to-day lives, we will be drawn in the opposite direction by our own sinful tendencies. The Holy Spirit's leading is not just AN alternative to the ways of the world. *It is THE ONLY alternative.*

> *"So I say, walk by the Spirit, and you will not gratify the desires of the flesh. For the flesh desires what is contrary to the Spirit, and the Spirit what is contrary to the flesh. They are in conflict with each other, so that you are not to do whatever you want. But if you are led by the Spirit, you are not under the law."* —Galatians 5:16-18

What is the fruit of being led by the Spirit?

Besides the obvious benefits of being obedient to God and walking according to His will, being led by the Holy Spirit also brings about a discernment and a spiritual perception that enables us to respond as Jesus did to the hearts (and not actions) of those He encountered.

Following are several statements indicating the spiritual perception Jesus was given as a product of His dependence on the Holy Spirit's guidance:

- *"At once **Jesus realized** that power had gone out from him."* —Mark 5:30 (see also Luke 8:46)

- *"Immediately **Jesus knew in his spirit** that this was what they were thinking in their hearts."* —Mark 2:8 (see also Luke 5:22)

- *"**He saw through** their duplicity."* —Luke 20:23

- *"Jesus, **knowing** that they intended to come and make him king by force, withdrew to a mountain by himself."* —John 6:15

- *"Jesus, **knowing their thoughts**, took a little child and had him stand beside him."* —Luke 9:47

Jesus' contact with people as He walked the earth was far removed from the casual interaction we are accustomed to. He seemed to be able to see right through each individual, knowing and responding to the motives of their hearts. But the more amazing thing about this is that you and I have been given this same perception through the Holy Spirit! Jesus made this clear to His disciples when they questioned Him about speaking to the crowds in parables. Look at His response:

"He replied, 'Because the knowledge of the secrets of the kingdom of heaven has been given to you, but not to them ... This is why I speak to them in parables ... In them is fulfilled the prophecy of Isaiah: You will be ever hearing but never understanding; you will be ever seeing but never perceiving. For this people's heart has become calloused; they hardly hear with their ears, and they have closed their eyes ... But blessed are your eyes because they see, and your ears because they hear." —Matthew 13:11-16

We all have been given eyes to see and ears to hear spiritually, which is a reference to the indwelling Spirit of God, but we must choose to walk according to the Spirit in order that we might also understand and perceive the things of God.

How are we led by the Spirit?

The working out of this baptism is not as mysterious as it may seem. The Holy Spirit speaks to us in the practical, day-to-day issues of our lives. It is not by a thundering voice that the Holy Spirit communicates, as some may expect. He speaks through our own thoughts and in a voice that is familiar to us. It is safe to say that every Christian has heard the still, small voice of the Holy Spirit within. The problem is that we often do not recognize it as such.

The Foundation Stones
  Doctrine of Baptisms

In order for us to experience the tangible presence of God in the person of the Holy Spirit, we must first acknowledge Him and His right and ability to lead us. Then we must practice REFERRING to Him in the currency of the moment. The Holy Spirit's direction is always fresh and new. We cannot assume that He will lead us today in the same way that He did yesterday. But we can know for certain that His guidance is always into truth.

> *"But when he, the Spirit of truth, comes,* **he will guide you into all truth***. He will not speak on his own; he will speak only what he hears, and he will tell you what is yet to come."*
> —John 16:13 (emphasis added)

Always keep in mind the character of the Holy Spirit. Scripture warns us that the Spirit is easily grieved by our choices (see Ephesians 4:30) and that we must be careful not to *"quench the Spirit"* (1 Thessalonians 5:19). In order to be led, we must be easily moved and willing to lay down our own agendas. But there is no higher calling in this life than to be directed and moved by the Spirit of God.

NOTES:

The Doctrine of Baptisms

BAPTISM	IDENTIFICATION	CHANGE	NEWNESS
Repentance	Holiness of God (God the Father)	Repentance (heart condition)	Preparation for Him (brokenness)
Water	Death, Burial, & Resurrection of Jesus (God the Son)	Actively Dying To Self (lifestyle)	Resurrection Power (life found in Christ)
Holy Spirit	Person of the Holy Spirit (God the Holy Spirit)	See the Holy Spirit (perspective)	Power to Live (walking in the Spirit)
Fire	Purity of God	Removal of the Dross (impurities burned up)	Drawn into His Likeness
His Body	His Local and Universal Body	No Longer See Ourselves as Separate from Others	Function as One Whole Body
Suffering	His Suffering	Loss of Self (heart change)	Many People Born Again
The Cloud	Leading of the Spirit	Move Away From Own Planning and Direction	Led by the Spirit (move with God's heart)

The Foundation Stones
Introduction

NOTES:

LAYING ON OF HANDS

The Foundation Stones
Laying On of Hands

LAYING ON OF HANDS

The **"Laying on of Hands"** is the fourth in the list of six foundation stones found in Hebrews 5:12-6:2. This is likely a practice with which most of us are at least vaguely familiar, but realizing its historical significance is crucial to understanding why it has been counted as one of the foundation stones of the Christian faith. And so we begin this study by referring to the Old Testament application of the Laying on of Hands.

> In the Old Testament, the Laying on of Hands was practiced for two very specific reasons, the first of which is the
> **TRANSFER OF BLESSING.**

If you have spent any time reading through the Old Testament, you might have noticed that blessings and curses were taken very seriously back then. We see blessings being transferred most frequently from father to firstborn son and always by means of the Laying on of Hands. While this particular blessing had much to do with tradition, it was also an actual prophecy from God over the life of the recipient. It was so prized that any deviation from the tradition (even by God's direction) was met with panic (see Genesis 48:8-22). The laying on of hands for blessing was an act of faith in transference, and everyone involved was mindful of God's sovereignty over their lives.

In the same manner, we find examples of the transfer of blessing from godly leaders (as they approached death) to their successors. At the end of the book of Deuteronomy, we are told that Moses died and was mourned by the Israelites. But God's presence and guidance did not depart with the death of Moses. Rather, it was bestowed on the one who would be raised up in his place—Joshua.

The Foundation Stones
Laying On of Hands

*"Now Joshua son of Nun was filled with the spirit of wisdom **because Moses had laid his hand on him**. So the Israelites listened to him and did what the Lord had commanded Moses."*
—Deuteronomy 34:9 (emphasis added)

Another way in which the transfer of blessing was realized in the Old Testament was through worship, the process by which we "bless" God. In Psalm 141:2, David wrote this prayer:

*"May my prayer be set before you like incense; may the **lifting up of my hands** be like the evening sacrifice."* (emphasis added)

And again in Psalm 143:6, David speaks of **spreading out his hands** to God in praise. Clearly the Laying on of Hands can be considered a sacrifice of praise when it is directed toward God in blessing.

> Secondly, the Old Testament speaks of the Laying on of Hands in regards to the
> **TRANSFER OF SIN**.

In Leviticus 4:29 and 33, we find detailed instructions for the Israelites regarding the Sin Offerings that God required of them. We are told that He who committed a sin against the Lord's commands was to bring a lamb or goat without defect to the priest to be slaughtered. Before the animal was killed, however, the transgressors were to *"lay their hand on its head"* (Leviticus 4:33) to symbolize the transfer of their sin to the animal. The slaughtering of the animal was then a means by which payment for their sins was made.

Later in Leviticus, we see another example of the Laying on of Hands for the transfer of sin. Leviticus 16:20-22 tells us of a practice in which the priest was required to *"lay both hands on the head of the live goat and confess over it all the wickedness and rebellion of the Israelites—all their sins —and put them on the goat's head."* At that point, the goat was not killed but released into the desert, so that it would *"carry on itself all their sins to a remote place."* This is where the term "scapegoat" originated. It is the taking upon oneself the blame of someone else.

While we wonder at these practices that are so removed from our day-to-day lives, there is actually great significance in these events as they pertain to the sacrifice of Christ. The Laying on of Hands in the Old Testament looked forward in faith to the coming Messiah. Christ was the Lamb of God, the unblemished sacrifice that took away the sin of the world. He assumed our sin and, like the scapegoat of the Old Testament, was driven outside the walls of Jerusalem to be crucified. God had a purpose in requiring what He did of the Israelites, however strange it may seem to us. The symbolic transfer of sin was meant to point them to the reality that was to come in Jesus Christ.

> *"But he was pierced for our transgressions, he was crushed for our iniquities; the punishment that brought us peace was upon him, and by his wounds we are healed."* —Isaiah 53:5

The Laying on of Hands took on a different dimension in the New Testament. Instead of looking forward in faith to the coming Messiah, New Testament believers (and all who have followed) needed only to claim the completed work of Jesus. So the Laying on of Hands today is simply the touch of faith to release what Jesus Christ has already done. The power is not in the hands themselves but in the faith that activates the promises of God. And Scripture reveals that this practice in the New Testament church also took on several different functions.

The Foundation Stones
Laying On of Hands

> In the New Testament, we find that the Laying on of Hands was utilized for purposes of
> **HEALING**.

Obviously, Jesus was the first to demonstrate the healing power in a touch of faith. His touch healed the ears of the deaf, the tongue of the mute, and the eyes of the blind (see Mark 7:32 and 8:23). Matthew 9:18 tells us that a ruler knelt before Jesus with this request: *"My daughter has just died. But come and put your hand on her, and she will live."* Jesus' healing power always responded to faith. There was (and still is) nothing beyond the healing touch of Jesus for those who had enough faith to receive it. It was not the crowds who pressed in around Jesus that experienced healing but the one who reached out in faith to touch the hem of His robe.

The exciting news is that Jesus commissioned this same healing power to the disciples He left behind, as well as to those who were yet to come. In the Great Commission (found in Mark 16:15-18), Jesus told us that those who believed would be able to *"place their hands on sick people, and they will get well."* And indeed the disciples healed many in the same manner as Jesus because a touch of faith was all that was needed to release the healing power Jesus secured on the cross.

> " *'He himself bore our sins' in his body on the cross, so that we might die to sins and live for righteousness; '**by his wounds you have been healed.**'* " —1 Peter 2:24 (emphasis added)

The Foundation Stones
Laying On of Hands

> The New Testament also communicates the importance of the Laying on of Hands in the act of
> **BLESSING.**

While we find little evidence today of the traditional family blessings that were so prevalent in Old Testament times, the significance of the blessing has not diminished. As a matter of fact, we are told in the Bible that Jesus went out of His way (much to the dismay of His followers) to lay His hands on and bless the children He encountered during His ministry (see Matthew 19:15). If Jesus Himself counted the spoken blessing as a priority, we can be sure that it still has its place in our lives as well.

> *"People were bringing little children to Jesus for him to place his hands on them, but the disciples rebuked them. When Jesus saw this, he was indignant. ... **And he took the children in his arms, placed his hands on them and blessed them.**"*
> —Mark 10:13-16 (emphasis added)

> The New Testament also shows the Laying on of Hands to be practiced in the
> **CHARGE FOR SERVICE.**

Acts 6 records the establishment of the first deacons in the early church, those who were given the responsibility and authority to oversee the practical provisions for believers. We are told in Acts 6 that the apostles *"prayed and **laid their hands on them**"* (v. 6) before they began their service in the church. We see this same pattern in Acts 13:3 where the Holy Spirit instructed that Paul and Barnabas be set aside for a special work. We are told that the church at Antioch *"**fasted and prayed**"* before they *"placed their hands on them and sent them off."* And so we see that the Laying on of Hands holds an important place in the charging of a believer for ministry.

> In the New Testament church, we find evidence that the Laying on of Hands was used in the
> **RELEASING OF GIFTS.**

In the apostle Paul's letters to Timothy, he claims more than once that Timothy's gifts were imparted to him by the Laying on of Hands. For example, Paul gives these instructions:

"Do not neglect your gift, which was given you through prophecy when the body of elders laid their hands on you." —1 Timothy 4:14

Later, Paul encourages him to *"fan into flame the gift of God, which is in you through the laying on of my hands"* (2 Timothy 1:6). It is not our place to know why God works in the ways that He does. But, just as He chooses to use the Laying on of Hands to impart healing and blessing, it is also a means by which gifts may be released in His children.

> Finally, the Laying on of Hands is practiced in the New Testament church for the
> **RECEIVING OF THE HOLY SPIRIT.**

When the early church was being formed, God sent His promised Holy Spirit at Pentecost. However, not all of the believers of that time were present to witness and receive His coming. The Book of Acts records that

The Foundation Stones
　Laying On of Hands

the Holy Spirit was received by these believers as well when the apostles laid hands on them (see Acts 9:6 and 8:15-17). It was the releasing of the gift promised to all who believed on the name of Jesus.

The Laying on of Hands is a very important concept in the Christian faith. It is the means by which God imparts life to us through fellow believers. But the Bible also warns us to be wary of imparting or receiving anything that is not of God. First Timothy 5:22 says this: *"Do not be hasty in the laying on of hands, and do not share in the sins of others. Keep yourself pure."* We are to guard our hearts in this area simply because the Laying on of Hands is such a powerful tool in the spiritual realm. If we are to walk in it, we must walk in it by faith alone.

NOTES:

RESURRECTION OF THE DEAD

RESURRECTION OF THE DEAD

Number five of the six foundation stones listed in Hebrews 5:12 through 6:2 is called the "**Resurrection of the Dead.**" It is often assumed that this term refers solely to the end of the age in which Christ promised to come back for his chosen ones. But there is a great deal more to understand about the subject and how it applies to our lives today.

The most obvious point of reference for this foundation stone, as we have already mentioned, is the context of physical death and the resurrection of believers at the coming of Christ. In 1 Thessalonians 4:13-18 Paul encourages believers to hope in the resurrection of *"those who have fallen asleep"* (v. 15) (or died) prior to the return of Christ. For we are told that the dead in Christ will be raised and caught up *"in the clouds to meet the Lord in the air"* (v. 17).

> *"Listen, I tell you a mystery: We will not all sleep, but we will all be changed—in a flash, in the twinkling of an eye, at the last trumpet. For the trumpet will sound,* **the dead will be raised imperishable,** *and we will be changed. ... then the saying that is written will come true:* **'Death has been swallowed up in victory.'** *"*
> —1 Corinthians 15:51-54 (emphasis added)

At that time, Christ will *"transform our lowly bodies so that they will be like his glorious body"* (Philippians 3:21) and *"we shall be like him, for we shall see him as he is"* (1 John 3:2). It is a promise that chases away all of the fears and uncertainty that otherwise surround death. We have good reason to look forward to our resurrection from physical death and our transformation into His likeness. In 1 Corinthians 15 (see above verses), Paul refers to the resurrection of Christ as the hope for those who have fallen asleep in Him. In 1 Corinthians 15:19, Paul says: *"If only for this life we have hope in Christ, we are of all people most to be pitied."* Therefore, the Resurrection of the Dead is the basis of our hope in Christ. It is because He was raised from the dead that we will be raised as well.

- **Death** – separation from life; loss or absence of spiritual life.

But there is an element of this foundational truth that we often miss. If we look at the meaning of DEATH, we will find that it touches two distinct areas. When we state that death is separation from life, we can easily understand how this translates biologically. But there is a SPIRITUAL DEATH that occurs when we are separated from the One who IS life. When Adam and Eve ate of the tree of the knowledge of good and evil, the consequence was death—both physical and spiritual—as God had warned (see Genesis 2:16-17). Every human being since then has been born into this condition, separated from God and spiritually dead. In Isaiah 59:2 we are told, *"your iniquities have separated you from your God; your sins have hidden his face from you."* Consider the parable about the prodigal son, in which the father represents God and the son represents mankind. Luke 15:32 describes the son as having been DEAD in his life apart from his father. Yes, he was biologically alive, but just as is the case with you and me apart from God, he experienced spiritual death.

Take a look at just a few verses that speak of the sinful condition that we are born into (emphasis added to the following Scriptures):

*"For the wages of sin is **death**."* —Romans 6:23

*"Therefore, just as sin entered the world through one man, and **death** through sin, and in this way death came to all people, because all sinned."* —Romans 5:12

*"The mind governed by the flesh is **death** ... The mind governed by the flesh is hostile to God; it does not submit to God's law, nor can it do so."* —Romans 8:6-7

*"Then, after desire has conceived, it gives birth to sin; and sin, when it is full-grown, gives birth to **death**."* —James 1:15

The Foundation Stones
Resurrection of the Dead

> *"As for you, you were **dead** in your transgressions and sins."*
> —Ephesians 2:1

> *"When you were **dead** in your sins and in the uncircumcision of your flesh"* —Colossians 2:13

> *"For since **death** came through a man, the resurrection of the dead comes also through a man. For as in Adam all die, so in Christ all will be made alive."* —1 Corinthians 15:21-22

The story of the Gospel reads almost like a movie script. It focuses on the utter hopelessness of a world condemned to death, condemned to eternal separation from God. And it sweeps full-circle to the moment that Christ would *"taste death for everyone"* on the cross (Hebrews 2:9). That is where Hollywood might roll the credits, leaving us in awe of the sacrificial love that was paraded before our eyes. Thank God, He did not stop there. If He had, the life and death of Christ would do little more than move us emotionally. Salvation of humankind would not even exist were it not for His resurrection from the dead. You see, the Bible tells us that WE died with Jesus on that cross. More importantly, we LIVE with Him through His resurrection. And that is why He came, to *"break the power of him who holds the power of death—that is, the devil—and free those who all their lives were held in slavery by their fear of death"* (Hebrews 2:14-15).

> *"We were therefore buried with him through baptism into death in order that, just as Christ was raised from the dead through the glory of the Father, we too may live a new life."* —Romans 6:4

There is another aspect of Christ's resurrection that we have not touched on. He paid the penalty for our sins, and, in doing so, He cancelled the death sentence that was against us. But we have to remember that we were also separated from God and spiritual life because of our sins. How did the cross affect our standing with God? Colossians 1:22 tells us that *"he has reconciled you by Christ's physical body through death to present you holy in his sight, without blemish and free from accusation."* We have not only been saved from the death that we deserved (**mercy**), we have also been given a righteousness before God that we absolutely did not deserve (which is **grace**). And this is the essence of the **Resurrection of the Dead**. It is not just that Christ was resurrected but that WE were resurrected with Him and given new life!

> *"As for you, you were dead in your transgressions and sins ... remember that at that time you who were separate from Christ, excluded from citizenship in Israel and foreigners to the covenants of the promise, without hope and without God in the world. But now in Christ Jesus you who once were far away have been brought near by the blood of Christ."* —Ephesians 2:1-13

John 10:10 (NKJV), a very familiar passage to most Christians, speaks of the purposes of Satan in the world—*"to steal, and to kill, and to destroy"* Jesus, however, claimed that He came to the world so that *"they may have life, and that they may have it more abundantly."* Do you suppose that Jesus would make this promise of abundant life—and in direct comparison to the schemes of Satan on this earth—if He meant it only for our life in eternity? He presents the resurrection life to us for RIGHT NOW and not just for the day of His return. It is not so important that we understand how the resurrection is going to spell out at the end of the age; it will happen whether or not we are knowledgeable about it. But the element of this foundational truth that God meant to be part of our lives TODAY matters a great deal. We have to realize that it is not just something to look forward to. It is something we must live currently.

> *"I tell you the truth, whoever hears my word and believes him who sent me has eternal life and will not be condemned;* **he has crossed over from death to life.***"* —John 5:24 (emphasis added)

The Bible makes it clear that everyone who is born again has been given spiritual life. Romans 8:11 says it this way:

The Foundation Stones
Resurrection of the Dead

> *"And if the Spirit of him who raised Jesus from the dead is living in you, he who raised Christ from the dead will also give life to your mortal bodies because of his Spirit who lives in you."* —Romans 8:11

As a matter of fact, Jesus claimed (in John 11:25) that He Himself **IS** *"the resurrection and the life."* Therefore, those who have accepted Him as Lord of their lives possess resurrection life because they are found in Him (see John 17:3 and 6:53).

> *"God has given us eternal life, and this life is in his Son. Whoever has the Son has life; whoever does not have the Son of God does not have life."* —1 John 5:11-12

What we need to understand is how the reality of this truth works out in our lives on a daily basis. While all believers have been given resurrection life through the Spirit, many never **experience** it in this lifetime. We can be free from death but choose to walk in it still, and God will allow us to. God's promises always work this way: we must possess them before they become real to us. If we do not, our life experience will be no different from that of unbelievers. The fact is that Christians need not ever touch spiritual death, but we do to some extent every day. The evidence of it is the fear, anxiety, frustration, anger, etc., that plague us. When we find ourselves in these places, we know that we have been walking separate from God.

> *"Therefore, since we have been **justified through faith**, we have peace with God through our Lord Jesus Christ, through whom we have gained access by faith into this grace in which we now stand. And we boast in the **hope** of the glory of God. Not only so, but we also glory in our sufferings, because we know that suffering produces perseverance; perseverance, character; and character, hope. And **hope** does not put us to shame, because God's love has been poured out into our hearts through the Holy Spirit, who has been given to us."*
> —Romans 5:1-5 (emphasis added)

The Foundation Stones
Resurrection of the Dead

As you may remember from our study on "Faith Toward God," faith begins by obedience to revelation. The verse above tells us that we were "justified" by our faith; that is to say that we were freed from condemnation and pronounced righteous in God's sight. Paul goes on to explain the pattern by which our faith is tested in order to produce in us perseverance, character, and, finally, HOPE. We live in a day and age where the quality of life has been lost; it is no longer faithfully passed down from one generation to the next. And the result is a lack of hope. We put our hopes in ourselves and others only to see them dashed at every turn. And God allows this to happen because He knows that there is no hope to be found apart from Him. **He is the author of hope.** This means that we are not required to muster up a measure of hope to put in Him. We must instead rely on Him as the **source** of our hope. Hope that is from God (through faith) is never disappointed. In fact, this hope stands completed already, for He has given us all things that pertain to life and godliness.

> *"May the **God of hope** fill you with all joy and peace as you trust in him, so that you may **overflow with hope** by the power of the Holy Spirit."* —Romans 15:13 (emphasis added)

And so we come to the matter of the Resurrection of the Dead, which is the backbone of our Salvation and the **hope of our souls**. If we do not possess this hope in our hearts—the hope that is not shaken by circumstances—then we have not responded to God in faith on this point. The resurrection life can be experienced only by faith, as Paul tells us plainly:

> *"I have been crucified with Christ and I no longer live, but Christ lives in me. The life I now live in the body, I live by faith in the Son of God, who loved me and gave himself for me."* —Galatians 2:20

Where the world uses the term "hope" with uncertainty, the hope that we have in Christ is a sure thing to be lived out **right now**. And, when we have placed our faith in God on the basis of His unchanging character, the hope that is generated becomes our stability.

> *"God did this so that, by two unchangeable things in which it is impossible for God to lie, we who have fled to take hold of the hope set before us may be greatly encouraged. **We have this hope as an anchor for the soul, firm and secure.**"*
> —Hebrews 6:18-19 (emphasis added)

Our hope is anchored in the fact that God cannot lie and that nothing is too difficult for Him (see Jeremiah 32:17-18, 27). What He has promised WILL be done in you and me because it already has been completed in Christ Jesus. We do not have to obtain hope, nor does our hope depend on our own abilities. What we have in the reality of resurrection life gives us abundant hope. Those who are spiritually dead consider life in Christ to be foolishness. The natural mind cannot comprehend the hope that we have. But we are no longer subject to the confines of our intellect. We have been given the mind of Christ, and we need only to abandon ourselves to His ability and character. Then we will experience and walk in the resurrection hope that is ours, which is Christ in us.

> *"To them God has chosen to make known among the Gentiles the glorious riches of this mystery, which is **Christ in you, the hope of glory.**"*
> —Colossians 1:27

And we will find that this hope produces within us an entirely different perspective of life. It causes us to be "eternally-minded," seeing all that happens to and around us in the light of eternity. The stresses of life come and go, but what we do in the midst of them has eternal ramifications. Second Corinthians 4:18 instructs us to *"fix our eyes not on what is seen, but on what is unseen, since what is seen is temporary, but what is unseen is **eternal**."*

> *"Since, then, you have been raised with Christ, set your hearts on things above, where Christ is seated at the right hand of God. Set your minds on things above, not on earthly things. For you died, and your life is now hidden with Christ in God. When Christ, who is your life, appears, then you also will appear with him in glory."* —Colossians 3:1-4

Hebrews 11, known as the "Faith Chapter," references several men and women of God from Abel to Noah and Abraham, and we find one common thread winding through their lives. Those who walked by faith in God *"considered him faithful who had made the promise"* (Hebrews 11:11) even though they seldom witnessed the fulfillment of them. But they were also looking at life through the eyes of eternity. In Hebrews 11:16, we are told that *"they were longing for a better country—a heavenly one. Therefore, God is not ashamed to be called their God, for he has prepared a city for them."* God calls His children to simply live by faith in what He has already done for them. And that faith must be based on nothing less than the faithfulness of God. This is our everlasting hope as believers.

> *"I am not ashamed, for I know whom I have believed and am persuaded that He is able to keep what I have committed to Him until that Day."* —2 Timothy 1:12

NOTES:

The Foundation Stones
Resurrection of the Dead

NOTES:

ETERNAL JUDGMENT

The Foundation Stones
Eternal Judgment

ETERNAL JUDGMENT

INTRODUCTION

"Eternal Judgment" is the last of the six foundation stones of the Christian faith as listed in Hebrews 5:12 through 6:2. While most of us are probably somewhat familiar with the idea of an eternal judgment, we often misunderstand its purpose, not to mention its prevalence to our lives today. Many believers consider themselves exempt from the consequences of their actions while others believe in a time of accounting but confuse their judgment with that of unbelievers. The Bible tells us that those who have rejected Christ will stand before the White Throne Judgment at the end of the age. Every evil thought and action will be exposed by the light of God's perfection. And each man's conscience will agree with the condemnation that he receives from God. It will be a time of great anguish, for God will cast out of His presence those with whom He never had a relationship, and they will be eternally separated from Him.

> *"Not everyone who says to me, 'Lord, Lord,' will enter the kingdom of heaven, but only the one who does the will of my Father who is in heaven. Many will say to me on that day, 'Lord, Lord, did we not prophesy in your name and in your name drive out demons and in your name perform many miracles?' Then I will tell them plainly, **'I never knew you**. Away from me, you evildoers!'"*
> —Matthew 7:21-23 (emphasis added)

This judgment is not a matter of determining what was done right and what was done wrong in a lifetime. Rather, these individuals will be totally convicted on the basis that they have rejected their Creator. And, because these never received the atonement for their sins, they will be held accountable for every last one. Proverbs 16:2 tells us, *"All a person's ways seem pure to them, but motives are weighed by the Lord."* And anything that is not motivated by a love relationship with Jesus Christ is counted as sin.

"The king will mourn, the prince will be clothed with despair, and the

hands of the people of the land will tremble. I will deal with them according to their conduct, and by their own standards I will judge them. Then they will know that I am the Lord." —Ezekiel 7:27

So where does that leave those of us who have trusted in Jesus Christ? The Scriptures make it clear that we **will not** be brought under judgment for sin as the rest of the world will, simply because it has already been paid for by the death of Jesus. Isaiah 38:17 tells us that God has put all our sins behind His back, so to speak. And in Jeremiah 31:34, God promises that He will *"remember their sins no more."*

"[H]e does not treat us as our sins deserve or repay us according to our iniquities. For as high as the heavens are above the earth, so great is his love for those who fear him; as far as the east is from the west, so far has he removed our transgressions from us." —Psalm 103:10-12

We can rest assured that our sins will never be held against us. But we will stand before the judgment seat of God all the same, and we will be called to give an account of our lives (see Romans 14:10-14).

"For the word of God is alive and active. Sharper than any double-edged sword, it penetrates even to dividing soul and spirit, joints and marrow; it judges the thoughts and attitudes of the heart. Nothing in all creation is hidden from God's sight. **Everything is uncovered and laid bare before the eyes of him to whom we must give account."**
—Hebrews 4:12-13 (emphasis added)

"For we must all appear before the judgment seat of Christ, so that each of us may receive what is due us for the things done while in the body, whether good or bad." —2 Corinthians 5:10

Keep in mind the analogy that Jesus used to describe the fruitfulness that comes with being rightly related to God. In John 15:1-6 Jesus presents Himself as "the vine" and His followers as "the branches." We are told that

The Foundation Stones
Eternal Judgment

God cuts and prunes so that we might be fruitful. But Jesus warned us that *"No branch can bear fruit by itself: it must remain in the vine. Neither can you bear fruit unless you remain in me"* (John 15:4). What we will be judged for is the SOURCE of our works, whether they were done in the flesh (apart from God) or by the Spirit. In this instance, however, the purpose for judgment is not punishment but **REWARD**.

> *"Behold, I am coming soon! My reward is with me, and I will give to everyone according to what he has done."* —Revelation 22:12

This is not a judgment to determine the authenticity of our salvation but the effectiveness of our walk with God. For those who walk by the Spirit and allow God to perform lasting works through them, there will be a sure reward in heaven. Ephesians 2:10 tells us that *"we are God's handiwork, created in Christ Jesus to do good works, which God prepared in advance for us to do."* We have been ordained (anointed and set apart) for good works (the purposes of God), and that is the usefulness that counts. What we will be called to account for is the fulfillment of these works that God prepared for us.

> *"For no one can lay any foundation other than the one already laid, which is Jesus Christ. If anyone builds on this foundation using gold, silver, costly stones, wood, hay or straw, their work will be shown for what it is, because the Day will bring it to light. It will be revealed with fire, and the fire will test the quality of each person's work. If what has been built survives, the builder will receive a reward. If it is burned up, the builder will suffer loss but yet will be saved—even though only as one escaping through the flames."*
> —1 Corinthians 3:11-15

The Bible mentions several areas of accountability according to which we will either be rewarded or suffer loss at the eternal judgment. As you read through these verses, ask God to reveal His desires for your life in Him.

The Foundation Stones
Eternal Judgment

STEWARDSHIP of ...

... Time ...

"Teach us to number our days, that we may gain a heart of wisdom."
—Psalm 90:12

... Money ...

"Remember this: Whoever sows sparingly will also reap sparingly, and whoever sows generously will also reap generously. Each of you should give what you have decided in your heart to give, not reluctantly or under compulsion, for God loves a cheerful giver."
—2 Corinthians 9:6-7

... Opportunities to Share Christ ...

"The fruit of the righteous is a tree of life, and he who wins souls is wise." —Proverbs 11:30 (NKJV)

"Those who are wise will shine like the brightness of the heavens, and those who lead many to righteousness, like the stars for ever and ever."
—Daniel 12:3

"Be wise in the way you act toward outsiders; make the most of every opportunity." —Colossians 4:5

... Gifts and Graces ...

"For this reason I remind you to fan into flame the gift of God"
—2 Timothy 1:6

The Foundation Stones
Eternal Judgment

RELATIONSHIPS

"Whoever welcomes a prophet as a prophet will receive a prophet's reward, and whoever welcomes a righteous person as a righteous person will receive a righteous person's reward. And if anyone gives even a cup of cold water to one of these little ones who is my disciple, truly I tell you, that person will certainly not lose their reward."
—Matthew 10:41-42

"God is not unjust; he will not forget your work and the love you have shown him as you have helped his people and continue to help them."
—Hebrews 6:10

SUFFERING FOR CHRIST

"Blessed are you when people insult you, persecute you and falsely say all kinds of evil against you because of me. Rejoice and be glad, because great is your reward in heaven, for in the same way they persecuted the prophets who were before you." —Matthew 5:11-12

"For it is commendable if someone bears up under the pain of unjust suffering because they are conscious of God. But how is it to your credit if you receive a beating for doing wrong and endure it? But if you suffer for doing good and you endure it, this is commendable before God." —1 Peter 2:19-20

PERSONAL DISCIPLESHIP

"Brothers and sisters, I do not consider myself yet to have taken hold of it. But one thing I do: Forgetting what is behind and straining toward what is ahead, I press on toward the goal to win the prize for which God has called me heavenward in Christ Jesus."
—Philippians 3:13-14

"Do you not know that in a race all the runners run, but only one gets the prize? Run in such a way as to get the prize."
—1 Corinthians 9:24

OVERCOMING TEMPTATIONS

"Consider it pure joy, my brothers and sisters, whenever you face trials of many kinds, because you know that the testing of your faith produces perseverance. Let perseverance finish its work so that you may be mature and complete, not lacking anything." —James 1:2-4

"They triumphed over him by the blood of the Lamb and by the word of their testimony; they did not love their lives so much as to shrink from death."
—Revelation 12:11

The Foundation Stones
Eternal Judgment

FRUITFULNESS

"For this very reason, make every effort to add to your faith goodness; and to goodness, knowledge; and to knowledge, self-control; and to self-control, perseverance; and to perseverance, godliness; and to godliness, mutual affection; and to mutual affection, love. For if you possess these qualities in increasing measure, they will keep you from being ineffective and unproductive in your knowledge of our Lord Jesus Christ." —2 Peter 1:5-8

"I am the vine; you are the branches. If you remain in me and I in you, you will bear much fruit. ... This is to my Father's glory, that you bear much fruit, showing yourselves to be my disciples."
—John 15:5-8

POSITIONS OF AUTHORITY

"Have confidence in your leaders and submit to their authority, because they keep watch over you as those who must give an account"
—Hebrews 13:17

"Not many of you should become teachers, my fellow believers, because you know that we who teach will be judged more strictly."
—James 3:1

These very things should be our passion. After all, what higher calling is there than to be an instrument of the Most High God? We were created with eternity set in our hearts, and we should be consumed by the desire to store up treasure in heaven. But we so often allow other passions to crowd our hearts, and our own comfort becomes our main concern.

In 1 Corinthians 9:24-27, the apostle Paul describes this earthly life as a race or competition. While the world runs for earthly, temporary rewards, we run *"to get a crown that will last forever. Therefore"*, Paul says, *"I do not run like someone running aimlessly; I do not fight like a boxer beating the air. No, I strike a blow to my body and make it my slave so that after I have preached to others, I myself will not be disqualified for the prize."*

We ought to run this race with eternal purposes burning in our hearts.

> *"Watch out that you do not lose what we have worked for, but that you may be rewarded fully."* —2 John 8

> *"If I discern in me a desire that cannot be satisfied on this earth, it must mean that I am designed for somewhere else."* [3]
> —C.S. Lewis

The Foundation Stones
Eternal Judgment

THE FEAR OF GOD

> *"Therefore, my dear friends, as you have always obeyed—not only in my presence, but now much more in my absence—continue to work out your salvation with fear and trembling, for it is God who works in you to will and to act in order to fulfill his good purpose."*
> —Philippians 2:12-13

God's purpose for warning us of the eternal judgment to come is that we might repent. We can find one example after another in the Old Testament of this very thing—God pronouncing a coming judgment against a people in hopes that they would repent and be saved (see Jonah 3:8-10). The issues of judgment should cause a godly fear to well up in us because we know that we will be called into account for the choices we are making today. But the fear of the Lord is not the same thing as timidity or cowardice. In the verse above, the Greek word used for *fear* means "reverential awe and healthy dread of displeasing Him." And this fear is meant to be a controlling motive in our lives for holiness.

The Bible tells us that the fear of God and His judgment is healthy. Look at just a few verses that pertain to this:

> *"And now, Israel, what does the Lord your God ask of you but to **fear the Lord your God**, to walk in obedience to him, to love him, to serve the Lord your God with all your heart and with all your soul"*
> —Deuteronomy 10:12 (emphasis added)

> *"Now **fear the Lord** and serve him with all faithfulness"*
> —Joshua 24:14 (emphasis added)

> *"**Fear God** and keep his commandments, for this is the duty of all mankind."* —Ecclesiastes 12:13 (emphasis added)

The Foundation Stones
Eternal Judgment

> *"Since you call on a Father who judges each person's work impartially, live out your time as foreigners here in **reverent fear**."*
> —1 Peter 1:17 (emphasis added)

Not only should we fear God out of respect and awe, but the Bible also tells us that those who fear Him are blessed.

> *"Who, then, are those who fear the Lord? He will instruct them in the ways they should choose. They will spend their days in prosperity, and their descendants will inherit the land. The Lord confides in those who fear him; he makes his covenant known to them."*
> —Psalm 25:12-14

Sadly, our generation has been deprived of sound judgment teaching. From the court systems to the local church to the home, the authority established by God has been completely undermined. Furthermore, humanism and the push for human rights have ushered in a spirit of **toleration**, and what the Bible labels sin is not even considered wrong anymore. The scheme of the enemy in this world is to cover over the consequences of sin and its effects. Our criminal justice system has failed to punish even blatantly sinful acts in a swift manner, and so respect for the authority of the law hardly even exists anymore.

> *"When the sentence for a crime is not quickly carried out, people's hearts are filled with schemes to do wrong. Although a wicked person who commits a hundred crimes may live a long time, I know that it will go better with those who fear God, who are reverent before him. Yet because the wicked do not fear God, it will not go well with them, and their days will not lengthen like a shadow."*
> —Ecclesiastes 8:11-13

If we fail to take seriously the punishment our sins may warrant on this earth, how much further removed does the judgment of God seem to

The Foundation Stones
Eternal Judgment

us? The world as a whole is living as if God does not exist. There is no comprehension of accountability, much less justice. But we can be sure that it is coming.

> *"Do not be deceived: God cannot be mocked. A man reaps what he sows. Whoever sows to please their flesh, from the flesh will reap destruction; whoever sows to please the Spirit, from the Spirit will reap eternal life."* —Galatians 6:7-8

We as Christians have to realize that we were not "pardoned" of our sins. Sin **cannot** be excused in the light of a Holy God. Those who do not receive the atonement for their sins that Christ provided through the cross will be left to pay an infinite debt themselves. When we understand the magnitude of what was done and the high price that was paid for our sins, we will experience the reverential fear of God. Our greatest desire will be to please Him so that we might be counted as faithful servants at the time of judgment.

NOTES:

The Foundation Stones
Eternal Judgment

NOTES:

Bibliography

1. Chambers, Oswald. (1992). *My Utmost for His Highest*. Grand Rapids, MI: Discovery House Publishers.

2. Hession, Roy & Revel (1997). *We Would See Jesus*. Ft. Washinton, PA: Christian Literature Crusade.

3. Lewis, C.S. (2001). *Mere Christianity.* New York: Harper Collins Publisher.

4. *Merriam-Webser Dictionary.* (1994). Springfield, MA: Merriam-Webster, Inc.

5. Strong, James. (1986) *Strong's Exhaustive Concordance of the Bible with Hebrew, Chaldee and Greek Dictionaries*. Peabody, MA: Hendrickson Publishers.

6. Vine, W. (1993). *Vine's Expository Dictionary of Old and New Testament Words.* Peabody, MA: Hendrickson Publishers, Inc.

7. Capps, Charles. (1976) *God's Creative Power® Will Work For You*. England, AR: Capps Publishing.

ABOUT THE AUTHOR

F. David Fawcett and wife Marian

DAVID FAWCETT pastored Cornerstone Christian Fellowship in Largo, Florida, for fifteen years. During that time, he took many trips to South America to share The Foundation Stones teaching that has blessed many people. He currently is an Associate Pastor at Liberty Worship Center in Largo and manages Destiny House, a discipleship training home that enables others to find freedom in Christ.

David and his lovely wife Marian currently live in the Tampa Bay area. They are blessed with three children and five wonderful grandchildren.

www.ingramcontent.com/pod-product-compliance
Lightning Source LLC
Chambersburg PA
CBHW060504090426
42735CB00011B/2102